THE ANVIL

THE ANVIL

by The Reverend
Joseph E. Orsini, D.Ed.

LOGOS INTERNATIONAL
Plainfield, New Jersey

All Scripture quotations are taken from the Revised Standard Version of the Bible unless otherwise indicated. Used by permission.

Nihil obstat:
   The Rev. Thomas Sharkey, J.C.D.
   Censor Librorum

Imprimatur:
   The Most Rev. George H. Guilfoyle, D.D.
   Bishop of Camden, New Jersey

THE ANVIL
Copyright © 1974 by Logos International
Plainfield, N.J. 07060
All rights reserved
Printed in the United States of America

Library of Congress Catalog Card Number: 73–93895
International Standard Book Number: 0–88270–089–8

Contents

THE ANVIL

· 1 ·

Introduction

THE icy rain slashed against my study window. I was slouched in the familiar cushions of my chair, and my mood matched the foreboding wintry night.

In the three exciting years since I had been baptized in the Holy Spirit and my book *Hear My Confession* had been published, the Lord had allowed me to see victory after victory in my preaching and in my ministry. But something was happening at the same time that was causing a feeling of distressful uneasiness—too many people were flocking to hear Father Orsini, too many were eager to be prayed over by Father Orsini. I was being touted as a healer, a prophet, a miracle worker, and the Jesus whom I loved seemed almost an afterthought in the minds of those desperate people who gathered to see and touch me. I knew it wasn't deliberate on the part of those enthusiastic throngs of souls. I also knew that it was dangerous, since both they and I could be easily led astray by a ministry that claimed to be full-Gospel, but shied away from the discipleship of brokenness and suffering. In spite of my public image, I was often overcome with weariness from my constant contact with sickness, hopelessness and demon power.

I knew I was not up to the task. And it was precisely at those times of weariness and weakness when the Lord's mighty power would break through. But again and again, Satan took advantage of my lack of experience and prideful nature. Under the pressure of tasks too great for me, I found myself becoming hypercritical. I began nagging my associates and spent less and less time in prayer.

I begged the Lord to change things so I would learn, truly learn, the wisdom of Saint Paul's request for prayer, "lest preaching to others, I too become a castaway." And the Lord answered that prayer. Immediately. Strikingly. Amply. The next day.

I was on official leave of absence from my diocese. A recent letter from my diocesan office indicated that my request for a year's extension would probably be granted, but there had to be an interview first. I drove the ninety miles to the diocesan office from my home, and when I arrived, the required interview took only an hour.

My requested leave of absence was extended until June 1. But I was informed that newly instituted diocesan policy deprived me of the right to exercise the priestly ministry while I was on leave.

The significance of the policy didn't hit me until I was driving back up the bleak New Jersey turnpike toward home. Suddeny I realized that for the next five months, I would not be allowed to celebrate Mass publicly, to hear confessions, or to minister in any way. At a stroke, all my public ministry had come to a dead halt. No more prayer meetings, no more speaking engagements—nothing.

When I realized this, I was tempted to rebel in some way. There were many ways to do so. I could defy regulations and continue to minister in secret. If pressure from my superiors became too intense, I could even leave the church and minister in some other denomination. But the Lord witnessed to my spirit, *Submit, obey, and be still.* And thus in the midst of a growing ministry, I withdrew. Not willingly, at first, but I knew I had to obey—or all that I had preached, all to which I had given witness, would be destroyed.

I write this message to share with my Christian

brothers and sisters in the charismatic renewal the difficult and deep lessons the Lord taught me from that February day to the present. I pray that these pages will help all who read them to learn what I have learned and to see what I have seen, in the lively hope that the *full* Gospel of Jesus may be taken to their bosom.

· 2 ·

Watch Out for the Thorns!

ALL that I had experienced and much of what I had heard and read in the charismatic renewal had been joy, joy, joy! Alleluia and glory!

No one told me to watch out for the thorns. But thorns there were, plenty of them, and they hurt.

The path *to* Pentecost is laden with thorns and sharp stones—the desperate searching, the wounds and scars of less than perfect human relationships, the disappointments of institutional Christianity, sin, and self-seeking. Although it is undeniably true that Pentecost is a mountaintop experience transfiguring and transforming the soul by the power of the Holy Spirit, the Christian cannot stay on top of the mountain in gilded tabernacles. He must descend, willingly or not, back into the valley of earthly reality.

Just as the path *to* Pentecost is laden with thorns, so is the path *from* Pentecost, but with this tremendous difference: Now the Holy Spirit is released in His fullness, and there is locomotive power on the pathway. Pentecost is the empowering of the Christian to live in the valley, to live out his dying to self, day by day, hour by hour, inch by painful inch.

When I arrived home that memorable February day, I moved slowly from my car to the little path leading to my front door. I observed the rose bushes along the path and clearly saw the dried-up rose hips, deep purple in color, rock hard in texture. Only a few months before, they had been glorious and fiery in splendor, bursting with delightful fragrance. The leafless bushes now showed, in stark relief, the ugly, sharp thorns previously hidden by green foliage.

"How much like my own experiences these past few years," I thought. What spiritual delights, what beauty, what joy, what victory had been mine! But now I was faced with the reality that I was about to enter a secret place filled with private pain. The awesome glory of Mount Tabor would now be balanced by the awesome loneliness of the Mount of Olives. I sensed that Jesus, ever the Master, the Teacher, would lovingly teach me that there are no worthwhile roses without thorns.

As I stepped into the warmth and familiarity of my home, my ears were greeted by the comforting sounds of my mother preparing the evening meal in the kitchen. I slipped into the living room, tears of disappointment and hurt already staining my face. I wanted time to control my emotions so I wouldn't distress my mother with something she couldn't understand.

It was a futile attempt. Mama came into the living room and looked at me intently. With that innate sensitivity of an Italian mother, she knew immediately that something was wrong. Then she sat down in a chair, and I moved over and knelt at her knees. Lovingly, she pressed my head against her bosom. Not a word passed between us, but she sighed deeply and began to weep for my pain. She didn't have to understand the circumstances surrounding the hurt in my heart. She knew with her spirit that her little boy was suffering, and slowly, just as her strength had made me grow in her womb so many years ago, now her strength again flowed into my weakness and absorbed my pain and frustration.

In those moments, the Lord Jesus taught me about His own mother.

In the evangelical and fundamental circles to which much of my ministry had been directed, the question most repeatedly thrown at me was, "Now that you have had the born-again experience and the Baptism in the Holy Spirit, how can you reconcile the Roman Catholic tradition concerning the Virgin Mary?" I had often used an answer attributed to the great Pentecostalist, David du Plessis: "The last recorded words of the Virgin Mary in the New Testament come from the incident at Cana, when she said, 'Do whatever He tells you.' Thus my devotion and veneration for Mary stems from her apparent role in the Scriptures—to direct us to obedience to Jesus, her Divine Son."

While I was on my knees that day, the Lord taught me that while du Plessis' answer was a pretty good one, it wasn't complete. The Catholic Christian devotion to Mary has been more cultural and human than theological and scriptural. The Mediterranean soil and atmosphere of the first Christian missionary effort, the Mediterranean tradition of veneration for the mystery of natural motherhood, was the source of the veneration and devotion to the supernatural motherhood of Mary.

Jesus brought to my mind the beautiful and deep relationship between Himself and His Mother; how she was always there, perhaps not understanding completely what her Son was about, but, nevertheless, trusting without question. What an example for all of us in our own personal relationships with Jesus! Although we do not understand completely the ways of God, yet we must trust, confidently and without question.

Oh the wisdom and compassion of our great God! He comes to us in the person of Jesus, through the totally human vehicle of Mary, and Mary through His grace becomes the model for our own deepening relationship with Him. What more human and easily imitated example could He have given us than His own lovely Mother? What son or daughter has not experienced, howbeit imperfect or limited, the total trust and love of a mother? No longer would I be afraid to declare my love and veneration for Mary, as I have never been afraid to declare the virtues and unselfish love of my own mother.

Thorns are a little price to pay for such beautiful roses.

My mother knew instinctively that no matter what pain and trauma I had endured earlier that day, her mother's arms and heart had begun the healing process within me.

Later that evening, I had to telephone my pastor, Father DelMonte, to inform him that I would no longer be able to assist him at the parish in celebrating the Lord's Supper and the other sacraments. He was distressed, of course, but he counseled obedience to the directives. His wisdom and experience became bulwarks against imprudent action on my part in the months that lay ahead.

As I prepared for bed that evening, I prayed that the Lord would strengthen my resolve to be obedient and submissive to authority, even if it meant total isolation.

· 3 ·

The Blessing of Misunderstanding

EARLY the next morning, I arose to celebrate the Lord's Supper privately for myself and my mother. It was a time of great blessing and comfort as we prayed together. The Lord seemed to say, *Don't fret! I have much to teach you. Trust Me!*

After breakfast, I began to contact all who would be affected by my withdrawal from public ministry. First I telephoned my brother in the Lord, Dan Malachuk of Logos International. Dan didn't quite understand the full significance of the new diocesan policy, but he promised prayer and support.

The rest of the day I dictated letters to my unofficial secretary, Florence Vayda. Florence, a faithful member of our Catholic Charismatic Prayer Community in Bayonne, seemed to have received the gift of tears. They always flowed abundantly at

11

our meetings, in prayer, while she listened to Bible teachings— This day her tears stained all of the correspondence necessary for canceling speaking engagements that had been set up all over the country.

That evening, I called an emergency meeting of the Pastoral team of the Bayonne Charismatic Community. At about eight o'clock, we gathered in the rectory of the Assumption Church.

The first to arrive was Brother Dominick Riccio. Brother Rick, as we all called him, rushed in with his usual dynamic enthusiasm and embraced me in his effusive brotherly fashion. When I caught my breath, I saw that Brother Carmen DeLucia was next in line for a bear hug. Brother Carmen, true to form, blurted out, "Okay! What's this all about?" Father DelMonte joined us, and we found ourselves wating—as usual—for Brother Ken Eliott, the only non-Catholic member of our Pastoral team. We often joked that he'd probably be late for the Second Coming. But we understood that Ken often worked late. Finally, he rumbled apologetically through the door, and the meeting began.

I explained as best I could what the situation was, and after the initial shock, accompanied by shouts —very human ones—of disappointment and recrimination, we settled down to pray and ask the Lord's guidance for the future of our Prayer Community. After some quiet time, I explained that we had to choose one of them to take over my position of leadership. The choice fell on Brother Rick.

I remember thinking to myself, "Poor fellow, now he's going to find out it isn't all glory. He'll have to be here early to set up the chairs, the book table, and see that all is ready. Members of the Community will come to him with their petty gripes and complaints. If anything goes wrong, he'll have to bear the brunt of the responsibility." I didn't envy him at all.

We ended with a decision to announce at the prayer meeting scheduled for the next day that I would no longer be in attendance at our prayer meetings because I had been called back to my diocese. It wasn't exactly a deception, yet it wasn't the truth, either. We should have had enough faith in the Lord and in our brothers and sisters to tell them the whole truth. We closed with an uneasy prayer, and sorrowfully took leave of one another.

I walked over to the church to spend some time in prayer in the presence of Our Lord in the Blessed Eucharist. It seemed to my lively imagination that the Lord began to remonstrate with me: *Why did you allow them to make that decision? And why this long face? Why allow them to feel that you are being unjustly persecuted? Do you enjoy being re-*

13

*vered as a martyr? Joseph, Joseph! You know
within yourself that you resent authority, and that
does not come from My Holy Spirit.*

"But Lord!" I bleated like a lost sheep, "But
Lord, I'm only human!"

*You're telling Me! I created you, remember?
And I recreated you, too. Your ecclesiastical superiors are not acting on whim or out of vengeance.
They have nothing against you personally. Don't
make this something more than it is.*

I was still for a moment, looked around the dark-
ened church, and riveted my attention on the Taber-
nacle again. After a few moments, I began to pour
my heart out:

"Lord, I know that this is an indirect result of my
book *Hear My Confession* being published without
an imprimatur. My superiors asked me not to have it
published because of a subtle attitude of disobedi-
ence to Church authority that seeped through some
of the last chapters. I regret that part of my book.
I really do. You know I attempted to prevent it being published."

A very feeble attempt, wasn't it, Joe?

"But I did try, Lord, I did! And what about
the hundreds of letters I received from ex-Catholics
and falling-away priests who testified that they came

14

back to the Church and the ministry because of my book?"

That's beside the point. Yes, I have used the instrument of your book to touch some of My lost sheep and shepherds. Nevertheless, aren't you forgetting that it was you who asked Me to change things so you would learn the wisdom of My apostle Paul's plea, "Lest preaching to others, I too become a castaway"?

"Yes, Lord."

Then be a good student and listen while I teach!

"Yes, Lord."

I slipped away from the church and drove to my sister's house. It was almost midnight, but after that lambasting, I needed some of her coffee and solid faith.

Evelyn was always astounding me with her unquestioning faith in the Lord. She attended our prayer meetings, and I had prayed for her to receive the Baptism in the Holy Spirit with the manifestation of praying in tongues. Her faith was a great deal stronger than mine. I knew, for example, that although her son, Frank, had been seriously ill many times, she had never given up. She simply believed, and through the Lord's grace, her faith literally prayed him back to health, time and time again. Evelyn amazed me that night, too. Her coffee was delicious, and her solid faith in the Lord against all odds was highly contagious. I was strengthened just by being in her company.

By the time I dropped into my bed, it was early morning, but sleep would not come. I tossed and turned, my mind churning with thoughts:

"Consider the blessing that misunderstanding will bring when through it you learn to recognize no hand but the faithful hand of your loving Father in heaven. You are giving far too much glory to the devil, the world, and the flesh, in the circumstances of your life. You blame your real or imagined enemies when you are in trouble, but great peace and quietness of heart will be yours when you refuse to recognize second causes in your life. God has been pleased to allow this to happen to you, and your part is to believe that 'all things work together for good to them that love God, to them who are the called according to his purpose' (Rom. 8:28 KJV).

"You find yourself in perplexity over being misunderstood. Rejoice in this blessing, as God is owning you as His son and preparing you for the comfort and blessing of others in the same trial of faith with the same comfort wherewith you yourself will be comforted of God (II Cor. 1:3–4). He is gracing your life with the glorious privilege of sharing in the most intimate sufferings of Christ (Phil. 3:10).

"Through misunderstanding, you will learn that the strength and grace of the Lord can be worked in your life only in the blessing of weakness brought to pass by the thorn in the flesh (II Cor. 12:7).

"The pain that you now experience will be transformed, by grace, into the goodness of God. Thus, like the trampled flower whose perfume rises to bless the foot that crushed it, so your own heart will find no bitterness, seek no revenge, wish no ill. The fullness of your own cup must overflow and bless those who misunderstand you."

A wave of great peace came over me as I began to praise the Lord in other tongues as the Spirit gave utterance, and at last I drifted off into untroubled slumber.

· 4 ·

Darkness before Dawn

IN that pleasant state between sleeping and waking, I was aware of a distant ringing. Over and over, louder and louder it became, until my mother's voice calling loudly, "Joe!" woke me with a start, and I realized the telephone was ringing. I hopped out of the pleasing warmth of my bed, and scrambled to the phone. Wondering who it could be, I picked up the phone and heard, "Joe, this is Father DelMonte. Could you come down to the rectory to see me right away?"

"Sure, Dom, what's it all about?"

"I can't talk now, just come down."

"Okay. I'll be there in about twenty minutes."

I dressed hurriedly and drove to the rectory. Father DelMonte greeted me and quickly got to the point:

"I just had a call from a Monsignor at the Chancery Office. He informed me that the Pentecostal prayer meetings we've been having for the past two years have to be stopped because no permission was ever sought or granted to have them in the first place."

I was stunned. I could hardly believe what I had heard. I looked at Father DelMonte and saw tears forming in his eyes. After a few moments, I found my voice:

"Dom, what are we going to do?"

"What can we do? We must obey. Let's call Rick to let him know, so when the people come for the prayer meeting tonight, he can tell them."

Brother Rick's reaction was stunned silence. He asked if he could call the Monsignor to clarify the directive, and we agreed that would be all right. Half an hour later, he called back and informed us that Father DelMonte had understood the Monsignor, all right. The meetings were to be stopped at once.

Rick agreed that we must obey, even if we didn't understand. That night, he met with the large group of people who had come for the prayer meeting and told them that the prayer meetings were being suspended until further notice.

A month later, we were informed that the directive had come as a result of a misunderstanding of diocesan policy, and that we could resume the meetings. During that month, the Lord showed us that all had not been well within our Charismatic Community. We found dissension, factions, and an underlying current of theological opinion inimical to the Catholic Church.

Because of serious doctrinal differences, two members of the Pastoral team left, taking with them many members. When the Community came together again, the full burden of pastoral leadership rested upon Brother Rick's shoulders, and in the course of a few months, the Bayonne Charismatic Community ceased to be. And in the deep darkness of the time before dawn, we began to learn some very important lessons.

One apparent lesson was that in any small charismatic group, deep foundations must be laid both in the Word of God *and* in the institutional Church. A ship cast off from its mooring soon drifts away aimlessly and becomes subject to the danger of foundering upon hidden rocks. Natural enthusiasm fanned by supernatural experience can lead only to dangerous postures unless it is tempered by a thorough grounding in the Word of God and a strong

21

link to the body of the institutional Church and to its invaluable experience. The Holy Spirit of God leads us not to fragmentation, but to unity with and in the Body of Christ.

We see in the Old Testament that even though the people of Israel consistently broke their Covenant with Yahweh, God did not leave them in order to go and form another people. Rather, He cajoled, He shook, He punished, *He* kept the Covenant. So in the New Covenant, inconsistent though His people may be, He does not leave them in their sin; rather, He cajoles, He shakes, He punishes—until they are transformed by the Holy Spirit into a people after His own heart.

The Lord God is infinitely patient in His mercy and His love. It is we, with our individual interpretations of His will, who separate from one another and claim God is "on our side."

I discovered from my own experience how easily one can convince oneself that he is right and everyone else is right or wrong, depending on whether he comes into line with our chosen posture. I myself almost became a victim of the alluring trap of personal cultism. If one is gifted with a "charismatic" personality and preaches a "popular" glory Gospel, he has little trouble in building a following. Better still, if he's consistently good enough, an evangelistic association preceded by his name will soon emerge, and finally, if time is on his side, a new denomination will make the scene. What a dreadful waste of energy to build a human temple of transitory glory!

The Lord is His wisdom and love acted swiftly to save me from myself, and in the process taught me that the charismatic renewal is exactly that—a *renewal* of a dimension that has always existed in the Church of Jesus. Revivals, movements, and renewals have come and gone, but the Church of Jesus has always remained—because the Son of the living God is the chief cornerstone.

The Lord taught me that His *full* Gospel must be taught and lived; if any *one* facet is emphasized to the detriment of the rest, then the wonderful balance of His life-giving message is thrown off center. The situation has a parallel in the laws of nutrition. If one consistently emphasizes one element to the neglect of the other elements, the body will eventually suffer disease. I am an active participant in the charismatic renewal—I love what the Lord is doing through it—but He has taught me that the Baptism in the Holy Spirit is only one part of His *whole* Gospel. It can be the starting point for many, as it was for me, but one cannot expect to win a race if he runs in place at the starting point and refuses to move down the track.

During the months that followed the cessation of the prayer meetings, my personal prayer life deepened, and the Lord led me out of the darkness of circumstances into the dawning light of His countenance.

What's So Good About Suffering?

MARCH was cold, blustery, rainy. The rain was almost maddening, day after day, seemingly without end. It was the kind of weather that makes people draw into themselves. The liturgical season was Lent, and the readings from the Scriptures assigned for the daily Eucharists I was celebrating privately, echoed the somberness of the weather, setting out in detail the sufferings of our Lord as He approached Calvary.

Time lay heavy upon me. After spending a few hours a day in study and writing on my doctoral dissertation, I retired to my room to be alone with the Lord. During this quiet time of withdrawal, I contemplated the role of suffering in the Christian's life.

While it is true that Jesus paid the price for our

salvation and we can do nothing to add to what He already paid, it is only fair that we *share* in that price, if we are truly His disciples. The Christian walk is tempered by shadows and rainy days. It has to be, for the life on which sun always shines will become dry and unproductive.

Jesus calls us to come to Him and live, but before we can live that abundant life, we must die to self. It is only when we are dead to self and alive to God that we are truly His disciples. God strives to make us lovable, and the process, a never-ending one in this lifetime, is often painful. In Malachi's prophecy of Christ, we read that He will be like a refiner's fire (Mal. 3:2).

After the initial enthusiasm of the Pentecostal experience with its ecstasy and glorious operation of the gifts of the Holy Spirit, Jesus, through His Spirit, calls each of us to a deeper identification with Him through suffering. It is at this point that many draw away in shock and disappointment.

We don't hear too much about pain and suffering in "charismatic" preaching, and that is precisely why the understanding of many charismatic Christians, especially new ones, is out of balance. Calvary's Cross is all right for Jesus, but please don't ask me to get up there, too.

What's So Good About Suffering?

The *whole* Word of God, the *full* Gospel, includes the important dimension of identification with Jesus' sufferings (Phil. 3:10). Pain moves men toward God. Consider the example of Job. Pain is an absolute necessity if we are to follow Jesus, because the human spirit refuses to surrender self-will as long as all seems to be going well. There are times when God wants to show us His vision of reality, but He cannot because our field of vision is already filled with our own desires. He wants to give us something, but we are too preoccupied and self-content. Then, at the very moment we think all is well, something happens to shatter our illusion. Pain teaches us that we can endure obedience to God and His appointed ministers.

A word of caution is in order here. By no means are we to look for pain or inflict suffering upon ourselves. God is not served by self-inflicted suffering. Guilt is not washed away by pain, but by the blood of Jesus. Saint John Bosco was criticized by his contemporaries because the rule of the Salesian Society which he founded did not impose self-inflicted penances like the other religious societies of his time. Don Bosco answered that the pain and suffering that God sends into every Christian's life are enough to effect His purpose. All we have to do is to accept, joyfully, what He sends, without trying to second-guess God.

Pain serves no purpose if it makes us bitter or produces a feeling of superiority. Once pain has taught us the lesson that God wants us to learn, and He offers us relief, we must not refuse it on the grounds that we are choosing to follow a "higher way."

There is the kind of suffering to which a few are called which can be explained only in the light of God's eternal providence, as expressed by Saint Paul when he wrote that all things work together for the good of those who love God and are called according to His purpose (Rom. 8:28). Only eternity will reveal the usefulness of some suffering. I am thinking of those precious Christians who are afflicted by either physical or spiritual suffering and whose faith is strong, but who never receive the blessing of healing. Peter tells us, "Beloved, think it not strange concerning the fiery trial which is to try you, as though some strange thing happened unto you: But rejoice, inasmuch as ye are partakers of Christ's sufferings; that, when his glory shall be revealed, you may be glad also with exceeding joy" (I Pet. 4:12–13 KJV).

The history of Christianity shines with those who have suffered with Christ and who in the end were the bearers of victory: "If so be that we suffer with him, that we may be also glorified together" (Rom. 8:17 KJV). These are the blessed ones who, with Paul, had no regrets in belonging to "the fellowship of his sufferings" (Phil. 3:10 KJV).

It is in the hour of suffering for God's sake that the believer shows the most intimate likeness of Christ. The Christian is called to suffer with God and for God. Jesus says to His followers, "You are those who have continued with me in my trials" (Luke 22:28).

There is a fellowship of Christ's suffering to which all are called, but not all enter. It is Christ within us who suffers and is continually persecuted. "If the world hates you, know that it has hated me before it hated you" (John 15:18).

Believers who fellowship in Christ's suffering seem to know Him in a closer, more intimate way. They stand with Him in His agony at Gethsemane. They hunger with Him in the desert and are tempted by Satan. They touch the repulsively ill with Him. They weep with Him over Jerusalem and the world.

I have had the privilege of knowing such a one, of sitting at his feet since childhood. My pastor, Father Dominic DelMonte, has been for me an example on one sharing the fellowship of Christ's suffering. I have seen him crucified over and over again by misunderstanding and neglect, but each time he grows stronger, and his identification with Jesus closer. He is one who has emptied himself for the sheep given him to pastor. In the midst of tribulation and sorrow, his face shines with the glory of Jesus.

As the dreary days of March hurried toward the promise of April, the rumors concerning my situation began to fly:

"He's been defrocked because of all that crazy Holy Roller stuff!"

"Oh! Father Orsini! Well, I hear that he's left the Church, married a nun, and become a Protestant minister."

As the rumors grew more and more ridiculous, Brother Pancratius, my "God-father," parried the blows. It had fallen to him to substitute for me in many speaking engagements. Poor Brother Panky! He had never imagined that this "God-son" of his would be so troublesome.

The incident that caused me more distress than any other at this time, was that many of the national leadership of the Catholic Charismatic Renewal at Notre Dame held me in suspicion because I had never made the pilgrimage to the annual National Conference on the Charismatic Renewal held there.

Brother Panky had to be my apologist and explain that I had never attended the Notre Dame conference because it was scheduled at a time when it was impossible for me to attend. He explained, also, that I was a priest in good standing, and the reason for the present silence was simply because I was being obedient to diocesan directives.

However, after some reflection, I realized it wasn't important what anyone thought. All I wanted to do was to follow Jesus as He led.

April came swiftly, and on Easter Sunday, I attended Mass in another city. The Lord comforted me with His presence and a sense of peace. Soon, however, something happened to disturb that peace once again.

When I was first ordained to the priesthood, I had taught Latin at Camden Catholic High School. One day I was standing in the hallway talking to another priest when I saw a handsome young boy, a freshman, bounding down the steps toward the lunchroom. I stopped him and reminded him of the rule against running down the hallways. He told me his name was John Panichella.

"Panichella," I repeated. "Do you know what your name means?"

"No," he said.

I told him that in Italian, his name could mean either "little bread," or "bread from heaven."

"Bread from heaven," I had thought to myself, and as the years passed by, that was exactly what John became in my life. For nine years, I watched him grow, and we became part of one another's lives. John was always a delight, and his loyalty never failed, no matter what the circumstances. He was my boy, later my man, and always my beloved disciple. And now he was to marry. The date was set for April 29. One of the most difficult tasks of my life was to inform him that because of my situation, I would be unable to officiate at his marriage.

This hurt us both very deeply, but the Lord used this hurt to bring us even closer. A short time later, I was privileged to lay hands on him and his wife, Phyllis, and watch them both come gloriously into the Kingdom through the Baptism in the Holy Spirit.

· 6 ·

With Strings Attached

IT was almost time for the end of my leave of absence. Looking forward to the day when I would be exercising the priestly ministry once again, I wrote a letter to my ecclesiastical superiors asking them to consider appointing me to a special apostolate when I returned on June 1. I requested an appointment as Diocesan Coordinator of Catholic Charismatic Groups. Because of my experience in the charismatic renewal, I felt I would be qualified for such a position. I could work full time at the job, overseeing existing groups, starting new ones, writing a weekly article for the diocesan newspaper, and conducting Charismatic Days of Renewal from parish to parish.

I received a considerate reply to the effect that I couldn't be appointed to this kind of position immediately, but that there was a chance for the future. At the end of May, I received my official appointment as Associate Pastor to Monsignor Michael Argullo at the Church of Saint Paul, Stone Harbor, New Jersey. I was delighted. It was a beautiful assignment, and I would be serving under a Pastor whom I greatly admired. I had been his assistant for a summer season a few years earlier and knew Monsignor Mike to be a man of prayer.

Early on the morning of June first, I said goodbye to my mother. Having lived at home for the past two years, it was difficult for me to pack up and leave, especially on my birthday. The ride down to Stone Harbor took almost three hours. When I arrived at Saint Paul's rectory, Monsignor Mike welcomed me with open arms.

I soon became accustomed to the routine of parish life, and I thoroughly enjoyed the warm friendship and support of Monsignor Mike.

He knew a great deal about the Catholic charismatic renewal. He had read my book, and one evening we sat together on the rectory porch after our evening meal and talked about it. Monsignor admitted that although he was not personally attracted to that type of spiritual experience, he saw great value in it. We discussed the possibility of starting a Catholic Pentecostal prayer group for the parish.

For the next few Sundays, I preached about the basic principles of the charismatic renewal. Many came to see me after Mass to ask where they could attend a prayer meeting, so we decided to begin prayer meetings at Saint Paul's. They were an immediate success. The Lord began to bless those who came for the Baptism in the Holy Spirit with the evidence of prayer tongues.

Then one day, I received a letter from my diocesan office which was a reply to a request for me to speak about the Catholic Pentecostal movement at an ecumenical gathering. The request was denied, and the letter implied that all such requests would be denied, at least for the immediate future. I accepted this decision without question, and realized I had to go a step further, so I suspended the prayer meetings. It was a simple decision on my part to obey not only the letter of the law, but also the spirit of the law. Everyone concerned accepted and respected my decision and continued to attend already established prayer meetings in distant areas.

During the month of August, I continued my parochial work in earnest and spent much time in prayer. I began to think about the role of obedience to authority in the life of the charismatic Christian, especially obedience to Church authority. I realized from my own experience that obedience is absolutely necessary for the complete peace we seek in knowing the will of God for our lives. As a professing Catholic Christian, it would be incongruous for me to use my Pentecostal experience as a wedge between me and those ordained by God to rule my Church. We are, I believe, called by Jesus to be an example of obedience. We are called to meekness, willingness to be trained for service, and to respond to higher authority.

Jesus calls us not to timidity or self-rule, but to obedience and submission to those He has set up in authority over us. The call to obedience is a shattering one, because the cost of obedience is the cost of dying to self. The daily walk with Jesus is a learning-to-be-made-willing process. Few of us are willing to do all God wants us to do, especially when God's will is made known to us by agents as human as we are. But we must be willing to be made willing. It is sad to see believers rebelling against God just because God chooses to rule His Church through this or that human agent. Jesus has recently become a popular example of a totally free, uninhibited being, and has arisen as the Superstar of liberated un-hung-up persons. It must be remembered that He represents the greatest example of servitude.

The charismatic Catholic must be a willing servant of God's Word, and a willing servant of His

Church. There can never be a conflict of substance between the two; at the very least, there can be a conflict as to method, as was evidenced in the discussions of Vatican Council II. Jesus left to those who would occupy positions of leadership in His Church some very definite instructions as to how they were to exercise the authority He would give them:

> You know that the rulers of the Gentiles lord it over them, and their great men exercise authority over them. It shall not be so among you; but whoever would be great among you must be your servant, and whoever would be first among you must be your slave; even as the Son of man came not to be served but to serve, and to give his life as a ransom for many. (Matt. 20:25–28)

It may be true that some have abused this authority, but the abuse of authority does not negate its validity. It is not to be rebelliously disregarded, rather it is to be prayed for until it comes in line with the intention of Jesus in its establishment.

God honors our prayers and our sacrifices. But above all, He seeks those who will serve, who will obey. He appreciates our obedience more than all our talent, more than all the astounding charismatic gifts that may grace our lives.

Thousands of Catholics throughout the world are

entering into the Pentecostal experience, and they are discovering that this experience comes with strings attached—strings attached to the discipleship of suffering and to obedience to both God's Word and the order that the Church rightly brings into their lives and experiences.

All Things Work Together for Good

ON September 25, I received notification that I was being transferred to the church of Saint Edward in Pine Hill, New Jersey, where I would be Associate Pastor. By this time, I had already received permission from my superiors to become involved in the charismatic renewal within the confines of the diocese. I was not familiar with the area to which I was being assigned, but I had been forewarned it wouldn't be an easy one for a number of reasons, one of which was that it was an economically depressed area.

The assignment did prove to be difficult. It needed a man with more pastoral leanings than I had. I asked to be put back into full-time high school teaching, because this was what I had been trained for. I had many years of experience, and I loved to teach teenagers. From the end of September until near the end of January when I was assigned as a teacher of religion on the faculty of Gloucester Catholic High School in Gloucester City, New Jersey, I caught a bad case of the Pine Hill blues. It was simply a case of the wrong man for the wrong job—a carpenter just does not feel competent to do a plumber's job. That's the way it was for me. But all things work unto good for those who love God, and this assignment gave me ample time to reflect, to pray, and to study. Much of my time was spent in putting the finishing touches on my dissertation, *An Educational History of the Pentecostal Movement,* and my study led me to meditate upon what Jesus was doing through the charismatic renewal.

God wants us to live in union with Him and with one another through Jesus Christ. We find this revealed in John's Gospel, chapters 14–17. God wants us to enter into that same kind of relationship which He has with Himself. Just as the Trinity is one, so does the Lord want us to be one with Him, the Father, and the Spirit. This is an amazing thing, an incomprehensible, beautiful, and loving fact. The Source of everything wants us to share fully in the life which He has with Himself. This is what man was made for. It is in our unity with God that we become complete. Creation, redemption, and the gift of the Spirit are all things which God has given to man to enable him to live with God. None of these things are ends in themselves, but through them, God and His creature—man—can live together, with man loving his God to his fullest capacity.

Jesus came to heal the breach between God and man and bring us together again in Himself. He is the full revelation of God to man, and in His Spirit alone can we come to union with the Father. It is the Spirit of Jesus which gives us the power to become the sons of God which He wants us to be.

> If a man loves me, he will keep my word, and my Father will love him, and we will come to him and make our home with him. (John 14:23)

We are all called to this union with God; there is no one whom He wishes to exclude. All a man has to do is to open the door to Jesus and keep His commandments, and the Lord will begin to draw that man to Himself and the Father.

In the seventeenth chapter of John's Gospel, Jesus prays to the Father that we may all be one —perfectly one, just as He and the Father are one. Jesus wants us to be His people. Just as surely as man was made to live in union with God, so too was

41

he made to live in union with his fellowman. God lives in unity, and unity is also the perfect and only way for man to live with man. Jesus says in that same chapter of John that it is our unity with one another that is the greatest witness to Himself (John 17:23). This may sound strange to some people, but it is true. Sometimes people feel that it ought to be the signs and wonders performed by Christians which show the Lord to be truly Lord. But practical experience has proven the truth of the words of Jesus. Many times people come to see a Charismatic Community and are totally unimpressed by the signs and wonders, the prophecies and speaking in tongues. What has touched them and has led them to seek a deeper life with the Lord has been the love and unity which they have seen and felt among the members of the Community. "This is my commandment, that you love one another as I have loved you" (John 15:12).

It is the Lord Jesus Himself who is the source of our love and unity with one another. We cannot love one another unless we have first let the Lord love each one of us. Many people make the mistake of thinking that they have a source of love in their own selves, that they can love another with a love which is their own. This is not true. All love comes from God. A love that hasn't first come from the source of all love is not a true love, a genuine love. Our love comes from Jesus, through us, to each other. Jesus says that He is the vine and we are the branches. The branches can bear nothing unless they are part of the vine. Paul says that Christ is the Head of the body. The body is nothing without the Head. Our love and unity is dependent upon our being grafted into Christ, becoming a part of His body.

In the Acts of the Apostles we find that those who believed "were of one heart and soul" (4:32) and that they "devoted themselves to the apostles' teaching and fellowship, to the breaking of bread and the prayers" (2:42). And again, that "all who believed were together and had all things in common" (2:44). These were all signs of unity and oneness in the early Church. This is how we begin to live our lives together as Jesus wants us to.

To many people, the early Church is too remote to be anything more than just a nice ideal, *not* something which can exist here and now. Some present-day Charismatic Communities, however, are experiencing the reality and beauty of community.

Every Christian is called to make total commitment of himself to his Creator and Savior. This step of totally giving oneself over to God is not just something God asks only of those who have reached a plateau of holiness. Commitment to the Lordship of Jesus Christ is a basic step for our Christian growth. Surrendering ourselves to Jesus Christ takes an act of one's will, deliberately turning to God, making the decision that says, "I am going to follow Jesus Christ and give my life to Him." Surrendering ourselves to Christ is something we must do every day of our lives.

This commitment to Jesus Christ is the first step for entering into the fullness of life as God's sons. We must be convinced that Jesus Christ is the Way, the Truth, and the Life.

Repentance is a second step. It is a deliberate turning away from sin and evil, the yielding of our human weaknesses and deficiencies to the Lord. Again, we must not fall into the error of viewing repentance as something we do just once. It is a daily act of turning away from sin and giving ourselves over to God.

Saint Paul speaks of repentance as a dying to our old self of sin and rising to the new life of Jesus Christ:

> We know that our old self was crucified with him so that the sinful body might be destroyed, and we might no longer be enslaved to sin. For he who has died is freed from sin. But if we have died

44

with Christ, we believe that we shall also live with him. . . . So you also must consider yourselves dead to sin and alive to God in Christ Jesus. (Rom. 6:6–8, 11)

On the Day of Pentecost, Peter spoke out to the people and instructed them on how they should turn to the Lord:

Repent, and be baptized every one of you in the name of Jesus Christ for the forgiveness of your sins; and you shall receive the gift of the Holy Spirit. (Acts 2:38)

Jesus Christ is the one who frees us from our sins. Jesus Christ is the one who delivers us from whatever bond of oppression or sin holds us back from living more fully in God's life and presence. We cannot free ourselves from self-centeredness and sinfulness. Only God's power and grace can free us. It is the power of God's Spirit which changes us and molds us into the image of Jesus Christ.

We must repent before asking to be baptized into the full life of the Holy Spirit. God's Spirit can fill us and work in us only to the degree that we are open to God and empty of self.

Repentance requires humility. To humble oneself is to admit before God that we are weak and sinful creatures and that we need God's healing power and strength to change us and make us whole in Him. Humility opens us up to receiving God's power for combating and overcoming sin. It opens us up to the Spirit's work of sanctification.

An honest appraisal of ourselves is necessary. We must look at ourselves and see where we are lacking and falling short as true sons of God. It is not enough just to tell God that we are sinful. We must confess before God all our sins. We must renounce evil and the sins of the flesh, the devil, and the world. Until we do so, we will be enslaved to them. Renunciation of sin cannot be complete until we make amends, where possible, for the wrongs we have done before God and men. We must strive to restore what we have taken and damaged by our wrongdoing.

It is not enough that we give up our ways of sin, but we must also forgive others, as God has forgiven us so much, time and time again. Finally, as children of God, we should gladly and unhesitatingly accept the Father's mercy and forgiveness. It is wrong for us to think that God would not forgive us, to fall into self-pity and refuse to consider God's mercy. God is slow to anger and quick to forgive.

These are important truths that God is teaching through the present outpouring of His Holy Spirit. I had ample time to think on them during my time in Pine Hill.

· 8 ·

Back to the Vineyard

MY new teaching job began on January 29. I had just returned from a pleasant ten-day vacation with my brother Toto and his children in the Caribbean. Refreshed in body and spirit, I arrived at school with a sense of eagerness and anticipation. It was wonderful to be back in the vineyard again, doing what I was meant to do. I was teaching three subjects—Marriage, History of the Reformation, and Eastern Religions.

When I arrived back at the rectory in Pine Hill after my first day of teaching, I was gloriously tired, but with the kind of weariness that felt good. I was back where I belonged.

I didn't tell my students that I was a Catholic Pentecostal, but somehow they discovered it and began to ask me questions after class. I answered them as best I could, giving them a brief overview of the charismatic renewal. I explained that God's incarnation in Jesus clearly demonstrated His interest in the world, in flesh and blood, and everything which belongs to human life. I told them that God does not merely express His opinion about human affairs; rather, He claims dominion over all the things of the world. He commands His disciples to advance to the ends of the earth, and He equips them with special abilities and powers for the mission.

We went on to discuss how God's reality and human involvement are again and again made questionable by Christians' weakness and silence. The world is waiting for proof of God's existence in the lives and actions of those who claim to be His children. And our God, who has proclaimed Himself the Savior of men, proves His reality through the things He does in this world.

Considering the history recorded in the Book of Acts and the Epistles, we saw that God's reality was self-evident to the first Christians. They knew no difference between holiday and everyday, making the first day of the week, then a working day, their special day for worship. They understood their Lord's commission to evangelize the world to mean not only bringing the Gospel to unknown lands, but sanctification of all areas of human life. If they met a sick person, they knew that they were called to pray for healing. In their communities, they dealt with the same kinds of problems which are still urgent today—racial integration, emancipation, consideration for the poor. These first-century Christians expected God's power to be seen in all areas of their world. The signs and wonders which accompanied the preaching of the Word were the effects and proofs of God's reality.

I reminded my students that the natural gifts were insufficient for transforming their environment and society. They recognized their own intellectual, physical, and moral weaknesses. But through the Holy Spirit, whom they had received at the beginning of their spiritual life, they knew they were powerfully equipped to be His witnesses.

"Christians today have the same task," I said. "And the power and gifts of the Holy Spirit are still promised *and* received by the disciples of Jesus. Because the problems of our times have grown to overwhelming proportions, we need God's power to prevent us from perishing in chaos and conflict. For this reason, He has sent us the charismatic renewal, so that Christians can express in their lives the reality of Jesus."

This was not exactly the kind of answer for which

my students were looking. They wanted to hear about all the "neat stuff," like speaking in other languages and healing. I tried to explain to them that these dramatic spiritual "fireworks" were only a part of the total reality of what God was doing in the charismatic renewal. I promised them that, in due time, we would discover together what it all meant, and they would hear about all the "neat stuff," too.

During the months that followed, I taught all the subject matter prescribed in the curriculum and the Lord also provided time necessary to give my students a thorough grounding and catechesis on the person and work of the Holy Spirit. Students came to recognize the action of the Spirit at work in the lives of men throughout the history of mankind. In the Old Testament, the Spirit worked through a few specific individuals appointed by God to be prophets, kings, rulers, judges, etc. In the New Testament, in the Acts of the Apostles, we saw the Spirit at work in the lives of all Christians, men and women, young and old. This outpouring of the Spirit on all men fulfilled Joel's prophecy:

> And it shall come to pass afterward, that I will pour out my spirit on all flesh; your sons and your daughters shall prophesy, your old men shall dream dreams, and your young men shall see visions.

> Even upon the menservants and maidservants in
> those days, I will pour out my spirit. (Joel 2:
> 28–29)

In several places in Acts are recorded instances
of the apostles laying on hands for the imparting
of the Holy Spirit: Peter and John at Samaria—Acts
8:14–17; Paul at Ephesus—Acts 19:1–7. Paul
wrote to the Corinthians:

> To each is given the manifestation of the Spirit
> for the common good. . . . For by one Spirit we
> were all baptized into one body—Jews or Greeks,
> slaves or free—and all were made to drink of one
> Spirit. (I Cor. 12:7, 13)

Jesus Christ had promised the apostles that He
would send the Holy Spirit to them. Until Christ's
redemption had been won for all men, the Spirit
could not be poured out on all mankind. It was
only after Jesus' death and resurrection that the
salvation of men had been accomplished and the
promise of the Spirit's outpouring could be fulfilled.

This outpouring of God's Spirit was meant for
all men who would believe in Jesus Christ, not just
in the early Christian communities, but for the
Church for all time. We can see the action and
power of the Spirit in the lives of many saints

53

throughout the centuries. Saint Francis of Assisi, Saint Catherine of Siena, and Saint Vincent Ferrer are among the notable charismatic saints.

Today, more than in any other time in history, there is an urgent need for the renewal of the power and action of the Spirit as at the first Pentecost. The Vatican Council was a summons for a renewal in the life of the Church. Pope John XXIII prayed that the Holy Spirit would pour out His works upon the whole Church as at the first Pentecost:

> May there be repeated thus in the Christian families the spectacle of the apostles gathered together in Jerusalem after the Ascension of Jesus to heaven, when the newborn Church was completely united in communion of thought and prayer with Peter and around Peter, the shepherd of the lambs and of the sheep. And may the Divine Spirit deign to answer in a most comforting manner the prayer that rises daily to Him from every corner of the earth: "Renew your wonders in our time, as though for a new Pentecost, and grant that the holy Church, preserving unanimous and continuous prayer, together with Mary the mother of Jesus, and also under the guidance of St. Peter, may increase the reign of the Divine Saviour, the reign of truth and justice, the reign of love and peace. Amen.

Pope John, *Humanae Salutis*

The charismatic renewal of the Spirit within the Catholic Church in the United States began in 1967. Since then, the Pentecostal experience of the gifts and fruits of the Spirit has spread among Catholics all across the United States and Canada and all around the world.

Jesus Christ is the one who baptizes us with the Spirit. When we pray with people and lay hands on them for the Baptism in the Spirit, we are making intercession to God for them, asking that Jesus Christ baptize them with His Spirit.

This Baptism in the Spirit is not an isolated experience, an end in itself. The Baptism is an initiation into the full life of the Spirit. It is the beginning of a totally new relationship with the Holy Spirit, the start of a new way of growing with the power of God, as our life begins to be reoriented and empowered by God's Spirit.

By viewing the Baptism in the Spirit within the context of the much larger picture, the total Christian life, we avoid picturing God's power as something static or something one just "gets" and "possesses." We see the power of God's Spirit as a dynamic force that works through time to change and transform an individual and a community more and more into the likeness of Christ.

The role of faith cannot be underestimated. It is the essential requirement to receiving the Baptism and the gifts. Faith is a stepping out for God. The Gospel account of Peter stepping out of the boat onto the water is an excellent example of this kind of faith. We cannot sit back and wait for God to hit us on the head with the Baptism in the Spirit. We have to put our faith into action and expect God to give us the Spirit.

Our faith is based on the promises of God's words. In praying for the Baptism in the Spirit, we claim Christ's promise, "How much more will the heavenly Father give the Holy Spirit to those who ask him" (Luke 11:13).

The Spirit wants to work in and through us and wants to give us His gifts for the building up of the Christian community, for strengthening the individual, and for equipping us for the various works God calls us to do:

> And his gifts were that some should be apostles, some prophets, some evangelists, some pastors and teachers, for the equipment of the saints, for the work of ministry, for building up the body of Christ, until we all attain to the unity of the faith and of the knowledge of the Son of God, to mature manhood, to the measure of the stature of the fulness of Christ. (Eph. 4:11–13)

A first step to receiving the gifts is having a desire for them. Saint Paul says: "Make love your aim, and earnestly desire the spiritual gifts" (I Cor. 14:1). God gives these gifts freely to whomever He chooses. He chooses those who are open and receptive to the working of God's Spirit.

Tongues is an important gift for the person seeking to enter into the full life of the Spirit. Paul instructs the Corinthians, "Now I want you all to speak in tongues" (I Cor. 14:5). The gift of tongues has a real value and importance for our growth as Christians. One important aspect of tongues is that it is a gift of prayer and a gift of praise. Every Christian needs to learn how to pray more effectively and more deeply. The gift of tongues can deepen a person's prayer life. Tongues can teach a person how to praise God. It is the Spirit within us, praising God perfectly. The Spirit also intercedes for us through this gift, praying to the Father for our needs and the needs of others, hidden even from ourselves (Rom. 8:26–27).

Praying in tongues is a means of growing closer to Christ. It is a gift we all need to have right from the start of our new entrance into the full life of God's Spirit. We should with real confidence claim this gift at our Baptism in the Spirit. We do not need to wait for this gift or shy away from it because of our unworthiness. It is a gift God gives freely, simply because we ask for it. It is not necessary that a person "psych himself up" or feel emotionally ready for receiving this gift. Three things are basically required: First, we should desire this gift; we should hunger and thirst for whatever God wants to give us. Second, we should ask in *faith* for this gift. Faith is based on the promise of Christ that He would give us the power of His Spirit. Third, we, ourselves, must cooperate with God by *speaking out* in faith and expecting God to give us the utterance.

There are some people who come seeking the Baptism who say that they don't want the gift of tongues. This is a wrong attitude arising mostly from their fear of making a fool of themselves by babbling incoherently. They are placing restrictions on God and His working; they are not really being open as God wants them to be. God wants to give these people the gift of His Spirit, but He wants them to accept Him on His own terms, completely and openly willing to receive any gift He wants to give them.

The lessons learned in receiving the gift of tongues can be applied to all the gifts of the Spirit. We must yield to the Spirit and cooperate with

God. God's Spirit will not work within us unless we allow ourselves to become His instruments. We have to use our bodies and our faculties in cooperation with the Spirit's manifestations of power.

· 9 ·

Eat All Your Spinach,
Or You Won't Grow Up Big and Strong!

THE months of March and April slipped by rapidly. I was totally involved in preparing classes, marking papers and tests, counseling students, and studying for the oral defense of my dissertation that would take place in May. By the time I arrived back at the rectory each day, the sun had already set. In the midst of all this flurry of activity, I often noticed that my spiritual batteries were wound down almost to the point of exhaustion. But there was always an evening's conversation with Father John Frey, the young priest who had taken my place as Associate Pastor, and this was usually enough to perk me up for the next day. Out of all possible priests the Lord could send to Pine Hill to take my place, Father John was really a gift from heaven. Not only was his disposition one of calm assurance, but he was also a participant in the charismatic renewal.

A great spiritual uplifting was provided once each month when I participated in a concelebrated Eucharistic liturgy with my brothers and sisters of the Camden Catholic Charismatic Community which met each week at the Church of St Rose of Lima in Hadden Heights, New Jersey.

Dr. Frank Iula was the diminutive but dynamic leader of the Camden charismatic group. I had known Dr. Frank from the very beginning of my priestly ministry, as he was my physician. Now, through the Baptism in the Holy Spirit, he and his wife Rose had become spiritual physicians as well, not only for me, but for the hundreds who came to the prayer meetings each week. Through our ministry to one another and to others, we learned the spiritual application of a common admonition we had all heard as children, "Eat all your spinach, or you won't grow up big and strong!" What our parents were telling us, in effect, was that although spinach seemed to be unappealing and unappetizing, the nutrients it contained were so beneficial to our growth and health, we should discipline ourselves to make it a regular part of our diet.

In the spiritual realm, the Pentecostal experience, the Baptism in the Holy Spirit, could be compared to the popular foods—pizza and hot dogs. Everybody likes pizza and hot dogs, but you can't make a steady diet of them and stay healthy. Other less popular foods, like liver and spinach, must be included for a balanced diet. So in the things of the Spirit, there must be a variety of elements to insure growth and maturation. The Pentecostal experience is the first thing on the spiritual menu, but what follows are equally important experiences to insure the proper balance of a healthy Christian life.

For many, the period following the reception of the Baptism of the Spirit contains a whole gamut of reactions and emotions, the result of a spiritual experience which leaves the person freer and happier than he has ever felt before. Next there may be the I-hope-it-lasts reaction, resulting from crowding doubts and fears that the Holy Spirit may be taken away if he isn't careful. Last, and most common, is a feeling of disappointment because the gift of tongues or some other gift has not yet been received. This disappointment does not necessarily mean a lessening of faith, but someone more mature in the life of the Spirit should take time to explain these things to the newly Spirit-filled Christians and to pray with them.

Each of those reactions must be dealt with tenderly and lovingly. Each newly baptized-in-the-Spirit Christian must be convinced that the "veteran" really understands what he is going through and be willing to talk and pray about it with him. This can be the special ministry of some who have been baptized in the Spirit and are committed members of the community—sort of a spiritual "buddy" system. The counselor must be careful not to squash the euphoria of anyone, nor demand more than anyone is able to give, nor brush off as unimportant or ridiculous the disappointment or doubts of anyone. God leads each one who is newly baptized in the Spirit, and the Charismatic Community's responsibility is to understand and aid that leading. Christian fellowship is the means through which the Lord leads these little ones to a closer relationship with Himself. There may be some "veterans" in the community who don't feel equal to the task. They should be reminded that if they are begging off because they discern a lack of maturity and wisdom in their own Christian experience, they should pray.

> If any of you lacks wisdom, let him ask God, who gives to all men generously and without reproaching, and it will be given him. But let him ask in faith. (James 1:5–6)

Both seekers and new recipients of the Pentecostal experience must be given a *realistic* and encouraging picture of what it means to grow in the Christian life. The Christian life is a life of balance and dedication to a deepening relationship with Jesus and other Christians. Dedication is important, for without it, the means of growth are of little value. It is for this reason, and from my own observation, that I have serious reservations concerning an indiscriminate ministry of the Pentecostal reality to teens and pre-teens. From what I have observed firsthand, it is only the exceptionally mature youngster who is capable of the necessary dedication indispensable for growth in the Spirit.

I have found many confused about what growth in the Christian life is all about. Many have been trained in a certain type of spirituality which says that being a better or stronger Christian depends on how much one does of or by himself. Many look at the great and popular Catholic saints as people who gave up many things and spent long hours in prayer and penance. Thus, the whole process of Christian growth has been conceived in quantitative terms— if you wanted to be holy, you had to *do* more for a longer period of time. But this is not the type of growth that was really taking place. It just looked that way to people who didn't understand what a particular saint was really doing. What was actually happening was a slow transformation *within* the saint—a death to self and a coming alive to Christ.

It is this death to self we have to undergo in order to become like Jesus. We must die to sin and to anything not seen in the person of Christ. It takes a lot of time and patience to become the person Christ wants us to be. The saints that the Church holds up to us as examples of what we also can become, didn't arrive at sainthood overnight. They sought the Lord every day and waited on Him *patiently,* because they knew it was Jesus who gave the growth and not something they did. Jesus leads each one of us at his own speed. He expects our *perseverance, patience,* and *trust.* A transformation is a hidden thing, and just because we can't see ourselves growing every day, it doesn't mean that growth isn't happening. We couldn't see the immediate results of physical growth from our eating that unpleasant spinach, but we did grow.

There are four elements necessary to the growth of a Christian. This has been borne out by the practical experiences of many in the charismatic renewal.

The first element is prayer. There is an absolute necessity to speak to God every day in prayer and allow Him to speak to us. This is how we come to know Jesus and the Father through the Holy Spirit. If we love someone, we want to know them in a more intimate way, and we naturally spend more time with that person. To say that we love God, especially after we have received the awesome blessing of the Pentecostal experience, and not spend time with Him in intimate communion, except at prayer meetings, is to say that our love is lukewarm. Love and communication must grow every day, and so we must spend time with Him every day.

Another element is study. One of the things which seems to come universally to people as a result of Holy Spirit Baptism is the desire to spend more time reading Scripture. This should be encouraged. God desires to reveal Himself to us through Scripture, and we should open the door for this avenue of revelation. God desires that we know Him fully and completely.

Some people have the problem of not knowing how to read the Scriptures. As the Scriptures came about by men prayerfully and faithfully recording what God had shown Himself to be, they should be read in the same spirit, *prayerfully* and *faithfully*. Commentaries may or may not be helpful, according to the natural intellectual abilities of the readers. Other books may be helpful also, especially those spiritual classics in the treasury of the Church's experience, and a discriminating choice of works by authors now involved in the charismatic renewal.

Another very important element in Christian growth is Christian action. The Pentecostal movement has been criticized because many of its participants seem to be inactive in important social questions. No one person can solve the problems of hunger, poverty, racism, war, and urbanization single-handedly and in one day. But neither will the problems begin to be alleviated unless the followers of Christ in this world seek out how to best accomplish the will of God in these areas. Our charismatic experiences do not absolve us from becoming involved. On the contrary, we have received the power to be witnesses to Christ and are thus given the tools to effect real and lasting change. A refusal to get involved in these crucial areas is a refusal to grow.

The actions we undertake should always be founded in prayer and in full accord with the will of the Lord. There are many committees and groups clamoring to get something done, but we must carefully seek God's guidance before joining them. The best way to approach the possibilities for renewing the temporal order is from the standpoint of the whole community. The whole community should support the activities of its members with prayer, active help, or encouragement. Any project which is from the Lord will find the strength and support of the whole Church community. Because Jesus has given us His Spirit, Christians have the power to transform the world for Christ.

The final essential element for Christian growth is community. In my experience, community or fellowship is one of the finest elements for encouraging Christian growth, because it is practical and down-to-earth. Charismatic prayer communities differ from place to place, but there are elements common and applicable to all. The way to become fully part of a community is to agree to have that special love and concern for one another which the Lord wills in the community. This takes definite commitment to attend the functions of a particular community. A person can hardly expect to be a loving and intimate member of a community if he is never around. I have seen many charismatic communities thrown into confusion by a lack of loving concern on the part of the members for one another.

People become integrated members of the community by submitting themselves to the discipline of the community. A community without discipline is not a community at all and probably won't hold together very long. If a person refuses to submit himself to the discipline of the community, then he ceases to grow as a member. The same thing is true in the relationship of the charismatic communities with the wider community of the institutional Church. Discipline within and by the community is very important, for without it, chaos rules, and the Spirit is hampered to move as He wills.

All of these ideas are spiritual spinach. Eat your spinach, or you won't grow up big and strong in the Lord!

· 10 ·

Where Does It Stop?

TWO of the students with whom I had direct contact, Pat Orsino and Jim Single, had begun to attend our prayer meetings. Pat was a lively junior girl. She became deeply involved in the whole charismatic movement and tried very hard to become an apostle to her classmates and friends. Through her, I learned the importance of being a responsible, loving, and generous servant to those whom the Lord leads to the Pentecostal experience. Just because a person begins attending prayer meetings doesn't mean that his problems have been solved; in fact, he continues to have questions and problems, and he needs someone to help him with them.

In my own experience, I had often asked the question, "Where does it stop?" The Lord had answered in His own way: "It doesn't!"

Jesus wants us to enter into a deeper relationship with Him every day. He wants us to become more and more as He is, holy and perfect. But man can't make himself perfect and holy as God is. God Himself must bring about our perfection, and He will if we let Him: "For God is at work in you, both to will and to work for his good pleasure" (Phil. 2:13). Holiness and perfection are part of a continuous process. "May the God of peace himself sanctify you wholly; and may your spirit and soul and body be kept sound and blameless at the coming of our Lord Jesus Christ. He who calls you is faithful, and he will do it" (I Thess. 5:23–24). Just as Jesus is the One who redeems us and baptizes us in the Holy Spirit, so too, He is the One who perfects us. Our part is to be patient, cooperative, submitting to His perfecting grace.

Graduation day is a big event at Gloucester Catholic High School. The most colorful part of the ceremony is the academic procession in which the faculty members, resplendent in the robes and hoods of their various academic degrees, join with the graduates in a glorious display. I had received my doctor's degree in the previous weeks, making me the holder of the highest degree on the faculty. However, because of a mix-up, my place in the procession was not the position of honor that my degree deserved. My dignity was wounded, but the Lord showed me it is better to trust in the Lord than to trust in earthly powers.

All that God has given us—our natural talents and achievements coupled with prayer and the spiritual gifts—was given in order that the love and glory of God might be revealed to men. As we grow in the use of the gifts of God, we begin to experience God in an ever deeper way. He is always with us. His hand leads and guides us. We become better able to hear His voice when He speaks to us.

Before my summer vacation began in the middle of June, I resolved that at least part of the summer would be spent in writing this book. As I prayed about it, agonizing over the prospect of spending long hours working on the manuscript, I began to understand that the more we come to know and love the Lord and live in His presence, the more we are willing to give our lives over to Him completely.

There may be areas of our lives which are not completely in the Lord. We may be unaware of them, or we may be painfully aware of them without knowing what we ought to do about them. The Lord wants us to be perfect and holy, and so He

73

points out these areas to us so that we can bring them unto the Lord.

For most of us, these areas turn out to be in the areas of obedience to Him and His Church, some secret sin perhaps, and priorities, things which we may still put first before Him. God has to be first in our lives—He won't fit anywhere else—and when we don't put Him first, He shows us through His Spirit. To use a biblical term, He "convicts" us. But God never shows us an area of our life which needs changing without giving us the help we need to change.

Jesus is the one who will ultimately overcome our trials, difficulties, and problems for us. Our role is to admit our weakness and to be patient while the Spirit works within us. Jesus ministers to us both directly and through the pastors of His Church, and leaders and members of our communities. The truth of this came home to me in a very clear way. I was at a prayer meeting at Saint Rose's Church in Haddon Heights, New Jersey, the new and permanent meeting place of the Camden Catholic Charismatic Community. During the meeting, the trials, difficulties, and problems that had been besetting me for so long seemed to almost overcome me. I fought against asking for prayer, in the falsely prideful conviction that too many present thought that I was so strong that they could always lean on me. But the Lord urged me to humble myself and accept the help which He was ready to give me. I finally broke down and asked for prayer. The result was a tearfully joyous release, a wonderful return to the feelings I experienced when I first received the Baptism in the Holy Spirit.

Where does it stop? It doesn't. The Lord continues to teach us forever.

Maranatha! Lord Jesus, come!

· 10 ·

A Solid Rock

A HOUSE built on solid rock withstands all the elements and remains standing. Many outside the charismatic renewal have viewed only its surface appearances and have judged it will pass away. Some of my own colleagues have tolerated my participation in the renewal and told me I would get over it as soon as the novelty wore off. It has been four years now and the renewal holds more meaning than it did when I first became involved. I would like to share with you some theological reflections on the nature of the charismatic renewal. The bulk of what I will say stems from the work of the eminent theologian, Killian McDonnell, from whom I have borrowed freely.*

* This chapter is drawn in substance from McDonnell's *Statement of the Theological Basis of the Catholic Charismatic Re-*

Those involved in the renewal have as their purpose the proclamation of the Gospel and the promised restoration of all men in Christ which "has already begun in Christ, is carried forward in the mission of the Holy Spirit, and through Him continues in the Church" (*Lumen Gentium,* art. 48).

The Catholic charismatic renewal has as its basis the Gospel of Jesus Christ. Those in the renewal wish to embrace without reservation the full mystery hidden from all ages in the Father, revealed in the Son, and demonstrated in the Holy Spirit. There is no other Gospel than that of Jesus Christ, crucified and risen.

Without wishing to absolutize the events described in the Acts of the Apostles, many see the central theological intuition of the renewal described in Acts. Jesus, crucified and risen, sends the Spirit. "Being therefore exalted at the right hand of God, and having received from the Father the promise of the Holy Spirit, he has poured out this which you see and hear" (Acts 2:32). Jesus both receives and sends the Spirit. The outpouring of the Spirit results in baptism (Acts 2:38), and the birth of Christian communities (Acts 2:41). These communities are built up by the teaching of the apostles,

---

newal available in leaflet form from Inter Faith House, Box 13, Louisville, Ky. 40201.

fellowship (koinonia), eucharistic celebration, and common prayer (Acts 2:42). Charisms appear among the apostolic community for the upbuilding of the Church (Acts 2:43). The experience of the Spirit's presence and power is directed specifically to witness and mission, and is related to the Lordship of Jesus (Acts 1:8).

Those in the renewal do not seek to isolate certain New Testament doctrines, practices, or charisms in order to give them a greater role than they have in the New Testament witness. The New Testament itself does not isolate the Spirit or His visible activity in the charisms from the other aspects of the Kingdom of God. Both the Spirit and His gifts are integral to the Gospel of Jesus and were accepted by the New Testament communities as normal parts of Christian life and ecclesial experience.

The renewal does not purport to bring to the Church something she does not have, but to bring her to release that which she already possesses . . .

Our hearing of the Gospel takes place within a tradition and history which have formed us and of which we are a part. The tradition joins us to the Gospel while the history separates us from the Gospel—as it was preached and experienced in the early Church.

The Church preaches the same Gospel that the early Apostles preached. But the renewal asks if the history out of which we come has not distorted our awareness and expectations so that our response to that Gospel has been diminished. For example, if our awareness of what it means to be "in Christ" and "to walk in the Spirit" differs from that of the early Church, and if we have more limited expectations than they did of how the Spirit is visible in the charisms for the service of the Church and the world, then wouldn't this have a profound effect upon the Church's worship, evangelization, and engagement in the life of the world? Those within the charismatic renewal make no claim to a special spiritual endowment, or grace, which distinguishes them from others not so involved. The difference is in their awareness and expectations—and therefore in their experience. The purpose of the renewal is not to bring to the Church something she does not have, but to widen her expectations.

If Catholic charismatics were asked in more specific terms to describe the theological basis of the renewal, they would maintain that theological research and reflection alone are not sufficient means to reach a final answer. The Holy Spirit, because He is "Breath," is less susceptible to analysis than Jesus, who is "Word." However, we will attempt to give some theological explanation that is, in the best tradition of Catholic theology, unashamedly sacramental, but which is offered without prejudice to other explanations.

The Spirit and the charism are regular constituents of the Church, not additions to an already existing body of Christ. In their absence the Church cannot exist. And it holds equally that no group or movement within the Church can claim exclusive hold on the Spirit and His charisms.

St. Paul defines the Christian in terms of both Christ and the Spirit (Rom. 8:9; Col. 1:27). In the Gospels what distinguishes the messianic role of Jesus from the role of John the Baptist is that Jesus baptizes in the Holy Spirit. In particular, by the sacrament of baptism one becomes a member of the Body of Christ because in baptism one receives the Spirit. "For by one Spirit we were all baptized into one body—Jews or Greeks, slaves or free—and all were made to drink of the one Spirit" (I Cor. 12:13). The New Testament describes in various ways the process by which one becomes a Christian —a process under the aegis of faith. The anointing of faith (I John 2:20, 27) precedes and accompanies conversion, which is a turning "to God from idols, to serve the living and true God, and to wait for his Son from heaven, whom he raised from the dead . . ." (I Thess. 1:9–10). Conversion leads to baptism, the forgiveness of sins, and the receiving of the Holy Spirit (Acts 2:37, 38).

Around these steps of initiation, and subsequent "walking in the Spirit" (Gal. 5:16), we can group many of the other New Testament expressions that refer to the process of becoming a Christian: baptism (Rom. 6), illumination (Heb. 6:4), baptism in the Holy Spirit (Acts 1:5), new creaturehood (Gal. 6:15), filling with the Holy Spirit (Acts 2:4), reception of the Spirit (Gal. 3:2), receiving the gifts and call of God (Rom. 11:29), entrance into the new covenant (Heb. 12:24), new birth (I Pet. 1:23; John 3:3), being born of water and the Spirit (John 3:5).

The coming of the Spirit that decisively constitutes a man as a Christian is related to the celebration of the Christian initiation (baptism, confirmation, Eucharist). The early Christian communities not only received the Spirit during the celebration of initiation, but expected that the Spirit would demonstrate His power by transforming their lives. Further, they expected that the Spirit would come to visibility in the community along the full spectrum of His charisms, which included, but was by no means limited to helping, administration, prophecy, and tongues (I Cor. 12:28; cf. Rom. 12:6–8).

The charisms of the Spirit are without number and constitute the means by which each member of the Church serves the whole body. Charisms are largely directed outward for the building up of the body and its service to the world. Less frequently they are directed inward toward the edification of the individual. Hence we can see the Spirit as He works in each Christian to make of him a servant to the Church and the world.

Unlike the early Church, the contemporary Church is not aware that all the charisms of the Spirit are real possibilities for its life. Its restricted expectations are in part attributable to its tendency to describe the assistance of the Holy Spirit primarily in terms of the hierarchical ministry. But whatever the reasons may be, if the expectation is limited, so will be the experience of the Spirit in the Church's life. And if the Church's experience of the Spirit has become limited, then so has its ability to give witness to Christ unto the uttermost parts of the earth (Acts 1:8). Hence spokesmen for the charismatic renewal maintain that there is an urgent need for the Church to widen its expectations of what the Spirit might do in its midst. They, however, do not wish to restrict the Church's theological and pastoral attention to the charisms per se, because they recognize that the gifts of the Spirit are not ends in themselves. Instead the charisms contribute to that fullness of life in Christ and the Holy Spirit to which the Church is called. The charismatic renewal, therefore, has its theological foundation in the celebration of initiation and calls for a renewal of baptismal consciousness broadly conceived, "That we might understand the gifts bestowed on us by God (I Cor. 2:12).

Questions Raised by Outsiders

The charismatic renewal is based on the assumption that the Holy Spirit is sovereign and free. He acts when, where, and how He wills. Though the Spirit takes persons and local churches where they are, He is not radically dependent on the subjective dispositions of those persons or communities. The Holy Spirit retains the initiative at every moment of the community's life.

I have already mentioned the more limited expectations of many in the contemporary Church in comparison to the wider expectations of the early Church. The normal experience of renewal inevitably causes the participants to turn their attention to the life of the New Testament churches. However commendable this return to the New Testament witness is, it should not be forgotten that in the course of the Church's history the Holy Spirit and His charisms have never been absent. The Holy Spirit has manifested Himself in a multiplicity of ways in various epochs of the Church. One could mention the lay monastic movements, the founding of religious orders, the prayer gifts in the Church's mystical tradition, the social awareness as manifested in the papal encyclicals, and the movements of political and social engagement. Though the modality in which the Spirit is manifesting Himself today appears to take a new form, it is inaccurate to maintain that the charismatic manifestations began with the Catholic charismatic renewal.

Tongues

While many of the charisms present no problems to persons not involved in the charismatic renewal, the charism of tongues does. The issue of the renewal is not tongues, and the Catholic renewal is not characterized by an insistence that speaking in tongues is in any necessary way tied to the spiritual realities received in initiation. On the other hand persons involved in the renewal rightly point out that this charism was quite common in the New Testament communities. Those who stand outside the renewal and attempt to evaluate the charism of tongues will fail if it is not understood in the framework of prayer. It is essentially a prayer gift enabling many using it to pray at a deeper level. If those within the movement esteem this charism, it is because they want to pray more effectively. For a sizeable number of persons who pray in tongues, this is only one of a number of forms of prayer. They also engage in liturgical prayer, eucharistic celebrations, and other forms of public and private devotion. This charism, whose existence in the New Testament communities and in early post-apostolic times is well attested, should be neither exalted nor despised.

Holy Spirit Baptism

Another feature of the renewal which causes confusion is the use of the phrase "baptism in the Holy Spirit." For historical reasons, many Catholics in the renewal have adopted this phrase, already current among classical Pentecostals, to describe the experience through which they came into a new awareness of the presence and power of the Spirit in their lives.

But there is a problem in the use of the phrase. It could be taken to mean that only those who have had a particular kind of experience of the Spirit have really been baptized in the Spirit. This is not the case, since every valid and fruitful Christian initiation confers "the gift of the Holy Spirit" (Acts 2:38), and "to be baptized in the Holy Spirit" is simply another scriptural way of saying "to receive the Holy Spirit."

Hence, many prefer to use other expressions to describe what is happening in the charismatic renewal. Among the alternatives which have been proposed are: "the release of the Spirit," "renewal of the sacraments of initiation," "a release of the power to witness to the faith," "actualization of gifts already received in potency," "manifestation of baptism whereby the hidden grace given in baptism breaks through into conscious experience," "revivescence of the sacraments of initiation." These are all ways of saying that the power of the Holy Spirit, given in Christian initiation, but hitherto unexperienced, becomes a matter of personal, conscious experience.

Whatever one may call this experience, it can happen without any emotional elevation. The experience, although it may evoke feelings, should not be equated with them. Further, this release or emergence of the graces of initiation into conscious experience can be a gradual process, without any strong emotional overtones.

Besides this growth pattern of experience, there is what might be called a crisis pattern. This occurs when one can precisely date the moment when the graces of initiation emerged into conscious experience. The crisis pattern is less familiar to Catholic theological cultures, but it is in fact common to many Catholics within the renewal. Both the growth pattern and the crisis pattern should be looked upon as authentic ways of realizing the graces of initiation at the conscious level.

Personal Commitment

There are many objective elements in the renewal as in the whole Catholic tradition: the celebration of initiation, obedience to the teaching and discipline of the magisterium of the Church, eucharistic celebration, the sacrament of penance, and the sacred Scriptures. But one of the most notable aspects of the renewal is its insistence on a largely subjective matter: personal commitment. As an adult, one cannot be a Christian by proxy. Each adult must say his own personal yes to the baptism received as an infant. This emphasis is in keeping with the more personal and explicit adherence to faith taught by *Gaudium et Spes,* art. 7. The constitution speaks of "a more critical ability to distinguish religion from a magical view of the world and from the superstitions which still circulate." This more critical ability "purifies religion and exacts day by day a more personal and explicit adherence to faith. As a result, many persons are achieving a more vivid sense of God."

One of the great strengths of the renewal is its insistence on a genuine conversion experience which leads to living faith, profound love of prayer, love of the Eucharist, new appreciation for the sacrament of penance, healing of interpersonal relationships, moral transformation, renewed sense of discipleship, awareness of the necessity of firm doctrinal basis, and fidelity to the bishops and to the Pope. In some places, especially in Latin America, involvement in the charismatic renewal has meant a new level of engagement in social and political programs. Pervading all these areas is the sense of the presence of the person of Christ, the power of the Spirit, and the glory of the Father. The response to His presence is, most characteristically, praise.

Conclusion

The strengths of the renewal may be instruments for the transformation of the interior life of the Church. Many people need a new assurance of faith and a renewed life of prayer. It is well known that many have ceased to pray. This is true even of priests.

The strengths of the renewal can lead to social and political action based not on class hatred, but love and prayer for the oppressors. This in no way lessens the struggle against the evils of poverty and violence. It means instead a more radically Christian style of social and political action wherein God's omnipotence is released to accomplish what men have failed to do.

A weakness of the renewal lies in uncritical acceptance of prophecy and tongues without sufficient discernment as to what comes from the Holy Spirit and what comes from the psyche. It should be remembered that the final judgment as to the authenticity of charisms "belongs to those who preside over the Church and to whose special competence it belongs not indeed to extinguish the Spirit, but to test all things and hold fast to that which is good" (*Lumen Gentium*, art. 12).

There is also present in some quarters an exaggerated supernaturalism with regard to the charisms, together with an undue preoccupation with them. This is evidenced by those who attribute too quickly to demonic influence a manifestation which is judged not to be of God. Then, in another sphere, there are those who imply that when one has the Gospel one does not need the Church. Over against them, and equally reprehensible, are those who oppose the subjective experience of salvation to the celebration of the sacraments. Another cause for concern is that insufficient attention is sometimes paid to the theological training of persons whom the various communities judge to be called to specific ministries. In fact, some place in false opposition the transforming power of the Spirit and theological training. One also laments the reluctance among some leaders to listen carefully to criticism —admittedly a nearly universal foible. Finally, some within the renewal have not drawn the inevitable social implications of life in Christ and the Spirit. In some cases there is social engagement, but it is largely superficial and does not come to grips with the problems of oppression and injustice.

An attempt has been made to formulate the most widely accepted view of the theological-sacramental basis of the renewal—a view based in the celebration of initiation. I have made some miscellaneous observations about the strengths of the renewal and about its specific problems. A final word should be said about the relation of the Catholic charismatic renewal to other renewals. Those involved in the Catholic renewal recognize that there are other renewals within other Christian communities and churches, as well as outside of them, which give quite different theological explanations for the same experiences. Even though the theological formulations vary, and even though the understanding of Christian revelation differs in important ways, those within the Catholic renewal recognize the presence of the Spirit in those who proclaim the Lordship of Jesus to the glory of the Father. That presence in all streams of the renewal is the bond of their unity.

· 11 ·

Is the Devil for Real?

MANY of those who have been involved in the charismatic renewal have long been aware of the existence and workings of the devil. But with the 1974 box office hit, *The Exorcist,* demons, demonization* and exorcism have suddenly become *the* topics of interest among the general public.

Informal exorcism or prayer for deliverance are ordinary occurrences at charismatic prayer meetings and the recent publicity given to *The Exorcist* have intensified questions concerning the actuality of the devil and diabolical activity. Since I am deeply involved in the charismatic renewal and have had some experiences with dramatic incidences of pray-

---

* This term more closely reflects that used in the New Testament than does "demon possession." See Frank Longino, "Demonized," *Logos Journal,* vol. 4, no. 1 (1974):19–21.

ing for deliverance, many have asked me to sum up Catholic thought and practice on exorcism. I believe that this should be done, especially to help dispel some of the false notions stirred up by the movie.

Father Donald R. Campion wrote in *America* (Feb. 2, 1974) "the Church has always recognized the possibility of possession, that is, the invasion of a personality by an alien spirit that seizes control of the personality and displaces normal human consciousness." He added, "although there are no instances of diabolical possesion in the Old Testament, there are a number of dramatic confrontations portrayed in the New Testament between Jesus and evil spirits who dominate another's body. Jesus is triumphant in these conflicts, driving the demons away.

"Similarly, there have always been Church rituals for exorcism, not only the extraordinary kind of ritual enacted in the film, but more familiar appeals that occur, for example, in the blessing of water and in the baptism of a new Christian."

The prayer of exorcism found in the Catholic rite of baptism follows a short litany invoking the saints on behalf of the welfare of the individual to be baptized. The new ritual directs the celebrant to pray: "Almighty and ever-living God, You sent Your only Son into the world to cast out the power of Satan, spirit of evil, to rescue man from the kingdom of darkness, and bring him into the splendor of Your kingdom of light. We pray for this child: set him free from original sin, make him a temple of Your glory, and send Your Holy Spirit to dwell with him. We ask this through Christ our Lord. Amen."

The Church has become increasingly wary of designating instances of demonization. Father Campion in the article quoted, explained the Church's reasoning: "this scepticism is based not only on increased medical and scientific knowledge, but also on genuine insight."

Linda Blair's graphic portrayal of a young girl possessed by a devil in *The Exorcist* is based on an actual case that occurred in 1949. The real victim was a fourteen year old boy, the son of a middle-income family in the Washington suburb of Mt. Rainier, Maryland.

From an account of what took place, strange things began to happen to the boy in January 1949. His bed shook and rose into the air, a rug on which he was standing slowly slid six feet and during the actual exorcism he raged loudly and shouted obscenities in unnatural sounding voices. Along with these signs, diabolical activity and infestation took place in the boy's room and home. There were strange scratching noises in the walls, at various times objects flew around rooms and furniture suddenly raised and moved itself. The actual exorcism took place in St. Louis over a two month period. It finally ended Easter Monday, April 18, 1949. The expulsion was so violent at times that it took ten priests to hold the boy down. Unlike the film in which two priests lose their lives, no priest died during the exorcism.

According to traditional Christian faith, demons are fallen angels who have rebelled against God. Their power is limited by God, but they retain the ability to act upon man and the material universe for their evil purposes. The form of demonic activity in which we are interested happens when a demon takes control of the personality of the individual person. Describing this in terms of a ship, the devil assumes the role of the pilot who steers the vessel. Pope Benedict XIV stated in a private opinion that "demons, in the individuals whom they possess, are like motors within the bodies which they move, but in such a way that they impress no quality on the human body nor do they give it any new mode of existence, nor . . . do they constitute, together with the possessed person, a single being."

Throughout history the Church has been reserved and cautious about reports of demonization. Such caution and hesitancy does not reflect a lack of belief in the reality of Satan and the power of evil in the world, but rather a desire correctly to identify where the evil is at work, what is natural and what is truly supernatural. For example, in themselves, spastic movements of the body or hysterical convulsions are not in themselves evidence that a person is possessed.

In the 17th century, a Jesuit theologian, P. Thyraus, gave four signs to determine the difference between the true demonization and natural mental phenomena. They are:

1. Revealing the hidden past or future events through the victim, which facts are shameful and scandalous in nature.
2. Speaking fluently in a foreign language the victim has never studied. (Here we must distinguish between the charismatic gift of tongues which produces the good fruit of the awareness of God's Holy Spirit and the counterfeit tongue-speaking produced by the devil with the effects of spiritual devastation—author's note.)
3. Levitation of the victim, uncontrollable body movements increasing the sense of presence of evil.
4. Telepathy and clairvoyance which bring humiliation and scandal.

Many authorities on the subject mention another criterion, namely, lack of memory as to what is said or done during the seizure. In other words, demonization involves suspension of normal human consciousness.

Cases involving the molestation of individuals, the bombarding of persons, their houses, rooms, furniture and animals have been recorded since the Middle Ages but the Church has never come easily to the conclusion that these have been genuine diabolical phenomena. The instructions of the old Roman ritual insist that every possible investigation be made for natural explanations before attributing such actions to supernatural or diabolical sources. The authorization of the bishops for the formal rite of exorcism demands exhaustive proof that the actions are not the result of natural causes. Fear-induced nightmares from seeing *The Exorcist* hardly qualify for formal exorcism.

The Church has always recognized the possibility of diabolical intervention in human lives, but insists that evil is primarily personal. Archbishop Leo Byrne of Minneapolis recently stated that "it is sin, not Satan, that is the root of all evil. Where Satan finds no complicity in evil through sin, he is powerless against us." (It is interesting to note that in *The Exorcist* the possessed girl is unbaptized and sinned against the first commandment by the use of the ouija board.) The main message here is that baptized Christians with a living and productive faith in the Lord need not fear Satan or his tricks.

With *The Exorcist* playing in neighborhood theaters, one thing is happening. Troubled people of all ages are calling priests because they are disturbed with excessive fear about the devil and possible possession. For most of these, it is unresolved sin in their lives that is the real problem. Jesus is the only solution to that problem.

Why the movie? Author William Peter Blatty expresses it this way: "*The Exorcist* was written to persuade those who do not believe that there is a case to be made for the supernatural force of evil in the universe whose game plan is to convince us that he does not exist."

So is the devil for real? The Scriptures and human experience say yes. But Jesus is real too. If our lives are truly and obediently under His Lordship then we have nothing to fear.

· 12 ·

A Personal Vision

MANY have asked me what I think about David Wilkerson's much publicized "Vision." Frankly, its content and the manner in which it has been publicized force me to suspend judgment as to its validity. I do, however, have my own personal vision of the future of the Charismatic Renewal, especially in the Catholic Church, with which I will conclude my book.

I see in the charismatic renewal today an increasing emphasis on the Lordship of Jesus—with the result that many Christians are beginning to reorder priorities in their lives. And this reordering of our own lives is significantly restructuring our Christian witness.

Once a person has accepted Jesus as his personal Savior and consciously decided to submit all areas of his life to the Lordship of Jesus, he is then led to participate in a Christian community wherein he experiences a sharing of the new life and the operation of the Holy Spirit's gifts. After a thorough grounding in the basic truths with the support of the community, the Christian is then led to serve his own community, and the wider community of the Church through a specific ministry discerned by himself or the community, *and* confirmed by the community.

A pentecostal Christian, then, is one who is living under the Lordship of Jesus through and in the power of Pentecost in a community of believers.

The Lordship of Jesus

Immediately following the first Pentecost, Peter preached a sermon in the power of the Spirit. As a result of that Spirit-powered preaching, his listeners were convinced of their own need, so they cried out: "What must we do?" Peter answered: "Repent, and be baptized every one of you in the name of Jesus Christ for the forgiveness of your sins: and you shall receive the gift of the Holy Spirit."

This simple message is the key we need today to enter and abide in the kingdom of God. But how do

I make this key work? What does it mean to come under the Lordship of Jesus? To repent? To receive the Holy Spirit?

Practically speaking, repentance does not mean so much remorse for past life or sins as a willingness to submit my life to the rule of Jesus. It is a decision to give everything I am, everything I have, to Jesus. I do this once at some point in my life, and I continue to do it as often as I realize the need. Repentance means to seek God first, and relying on Him to take care of the practical details of life.

But how do I know if repentance is needed? Simply by asking myself these questions:

1. Who is first in my life?
   a. Is it myself?
   b. Is it my wife or husband?
   c. Is it my children?
   d. Is it my parents?
   e. Is it someone else I feel I love and can't give up?

   or is it Jesus???

2. How do I find out who is first in my life? Simple. What or who fills my imagination most? With what or whom do I spend most of my time? Not the time I must spend at my job or

duties, but my *free time?* Where and on what do I spend my own personal money?

If I find that Jesus is not first in my life, in *all* areas of my life including my relationships with others, my thoughts, my imagination, my sexuality, what must I do? Every day I must make a conscious act of submission to Jesus. I must have enough boldness of faith to say: "Here I am, Lord! Take me! I give You all that I am."

In the daily living of repentance, I must trust that the Holy Spirit will convict me of sin in those areas of my life that I have not yielded completely or that need daily yielding to the Lord. How will this take place? Wherever I lose my peace—that is where I find sin. In Galatians 5, Paul describes the criteria for the normal Christian life, the fruits of the Spirit: love, peace, faithfulness, kindness, joy, patience, meekness, gentleness and self-control. Whenever these are missing, there is sin, and the Holy Spirit is calling me to submit that area of unrest to the Lordship of Jesus.

As Pentecostals, we claim that we have received the Baptism in the Holy Spirit. This means that we have consciously and deliberately sought for the release of the Holy Spirit and His power in our lives. As a result, the Holy Spirit has manifested His possession of us through the operation of the spiritual gifts (tongues, healing, prophecy, etc.). But yielding to the will of the Holy Spirit is not a one-shot deal. Certainly we receive the Baptism in the Spirit once we ask for it, and experience its effects in proportion to how much we have yielded at the time; but yielding to the Spirit is a continuing experience, a daily release of His power, a continual Baptism in the Spirit.

Yielding to the Holy Spirit leads us into the eternal childhood of believers. "Unless you become like little children, you shall not enter the kingdom." This requirement deeply challenges the American ideal of independence: "I'd rather do it myself!" It means becoming as dependent as an infant in the things of the Lord. It is the heartfelt prayer of one who knows he is helpless, "You lead me, Lord!" It means waiting on the Holy Spirit so that my speaking in tongues, prophecy or interpretation are authentic. On the other side of the same coin is a faith-principle that must be in operation lest we fall into the error of quietism. It says, "You get as much as you expect." While we passively wait on the Lord in a certain circumstance, that passivity must be set in an active faith that says, "I believe the Lord will lead me, and when He does, I will obey." We must become participants in a continuing process of basic initiation as an ongoing feature of our Christian communities. There is no better method than the one found in the Scriptures:

Kerygma*

Proclaim the Gospel—Jesus is Lord! Our Christian communities must become centers for the study and practice of the Word of God. A very useful tool to begin the process is a "Life in the Spirit Seminar" taught by a revolving team of teachers who teach what they have learned. The lessons must be practical, concrete, and find living expression in the lives of those teaching. An old Latin adage sums it up: *nemo dat quod non habet,* "no one can give what he doesn't have." This means that those who fulfill the teaching role in the proclamation of the Word had better be living what they proclaim. We must acknowledge that the majority of nominal Christians have not been evangelized, and many others have not so much as heard the full Gospel message. So our primary task is to evangelize families, friends, and fellow church members. These are people who have known us too well. For most of them the most effective evangelization will consist of the Gospel

---

* *Kerygma* is a Greek word that means *proclamation* or *announcement* (commonly pronounced kah-*rig*-mah).

they see changing us, our actions and our attitudes. If and when they *see* the truth of the Good News lived in us, then perhaps they will be more easily convinced of its reality.

Didache*

In *didache* the information passed on through the *kerygma* is appropriated. The Lordship and redemption of Jesus is personally made an integral part and center of the Christian's life. This appropriation takes place when the neophyte, the newly re-born and Spirit-baptized Christian, enters into serious relationship with a group of those who have been living the new life for some time. It is in and through the small growth group that the neophyte begins to see the implications of Christ's reign in his life by observing the lives of his brothers and sisters and listening to their advice. An excellent tool to present the basic principles to be learned and appropriated during this growth period are the "Founations Courses I and II" prepared by the New Life Community in Ann Arbor, Michigan.

* *Didache* is a Greek word that means *teaching* or *instruction* (commonly pronounced *di*-dah-kay).

Discipleship

Ordinarily, we judge that a person is a believer if he does three things:

a. Attends church services regularly;
b. Supports his church financially;
c. Tries to live a holy life.

But these criteria would be the same for the member of any club. Isn't the Church more than a club? Isn't it the Body of Christ? A believer is a member of a body not simply a club. Biology tells us that a member of the body takes in life and passes it on through circulation and cell production under the direction of the nervous system, controlled by the brain. It is the same in the Body of Christ. We as members take in life, His life, and reproduce ourselves by passing on that life under direction from the Head. Christ's last command was, "Go, therefore and make disciples of all nations . . . !" A disciple is one who is taught (*kerygma*) and formed (*didache*) so that he may teach and form others under Christ's direction. When St. Paul wrote, "Imitate me," he was not being proud. He knew it was the pattern God had ordained. Real discipling cannot be accomplished with throngs of people. The

108

Lord Himself evangelized thousands, but discipled only twelve. Those twelve, in turn, discipled a further seventy-two.

This means that priests and lay leaders in the Catholic charismatic renewal must curtail their leadership roles with large groups and concentrate on smaller ones. This is taking one step backward so as to be able to take two steps forward. Leaders in the charismatic renewal will increasingly find their energies dissipated unless they are willing to commit themselves to a few rather than to many. This will constitute a sore blow to the sense of self-importance that plagues most leaders. They must refuse to become involved in outside interests no matter how "charismatic." They must further realize that they are not the star of the show. Jesus is the only star and He will accomplish His ministry through His Body. Discipleship is the most time-consuming and trying way to build that Body, but it is Christ's way.

A priest or layman who has emerged as a leader in a prayer group should pick a few disciples only after much prayer and reflection. He should enter into serious covenant with them and, under the Headship of Christ, share with them, intimately and candidly, what God has taught him by real experience—not by books. In time, these budding disciples

109

will have experienced some things themselves and be ready to "teach others also." As discipleship grows, so will the Body, solidly and soundly.

Such discipling cells must be squarely under the authority of the local church; that is probably one good reason to nurture leadership in the priests, so that the whole work may tie the movement in with the institutional church. In this way we can begin to see the total vision of the whole Church charismatically renewed both in structure and operation.

The implications of this basic message for the whole Church are unlimited. Local churches could be entirely restructured according to the pattern of evangelization, formation, and discipleship. Pastors and priests could be transformed by the Spirit and take up the task of living and preaching the Gospel no longer caught up in bureaucratic detail and the vain effort to raise funds from uncommitted, unevangelized, and nominal Christians. Evangelized, Spirit-filled Christians don't have to be persuaded or coerced by professional fund-raisers to support the life and works of the Church. Such giving is merely the logical expression of genuine discipleship. The ordinary parishioner can become totally involved in the proclamation of the Gospel through his own experience of it, and the ongoing experience of the gifts and fruits of the Spirit. Imagine the office of Apostle-Bishop, the presbyterate, and the parish renewed by the Spirit in terms of evangelization, formation, and discipleship. Imagine Catholic education being restructured according to the scriptural model of *kerygma, didache,* and discipleship. The final purpose of the charismatic renewal is not to form permanent prayer groups, but alternate supportive non-permanent communities which will facilitate the restructuring of Christian institution to enliven and broaden the Body of Christ. This is the long-range goal of the charismatic renewal. We must be committed to work toward it. Meanwhile, our immediate commitment is undoubtedly to evangelization—telling and living the Good News. By obeying the Spirit one step at a time we will see the total vision come about in God's way at God's time.

7-74

Now you can hear famous authors . . . recorded live . . .
telling of a personal experience or testimony

CASSETTES

_____	ARGUINZONI, SONNY—God's Junkie	TA17	3.95
_____	BARTLETT, BOB—The Soul Patrol	TA6X	3.95
_____	BENNETT, DENNIS—Nine O'Clock in The Morning	TA5X	3.95
_____	BJORNSTADT, JAMES—20th Century Prophecy	JB1X	3.95
_____	BREDESEN, ROBERTS—Charismatic Renewal	TA22	3.95
_____	BUCKINGHAM, JAMIE—Some Gall	TA3X	3.95
_____	CANTELON, WILLARD—Day The Dollar Dies	TA21	3.95
_____	CAROTHERS, MERLIN—Prison to Praise	TA2X	3.95
_____	CHRISTIANSON, CHRIS—God Did Not Ordain Silence	TA37	3.95
_____	CORNWALL, JUDSON—Let Us Praise	TA31	3.95
_____	CRUZ, NICKY—Run Baby Run	TA1X	3.95
_____	duPLESSIS, DAVID—The Spirit Bade Me Go	TA11	3.95
_____	DURASOFF, STEVE—Pent. Behind Iron Curtain	TA30	3.95
_____	ERVIN, HOWARD—These Are Not Drunken	TA13	3.95
_____	ESSES, MIKE—Michael, Michael	TA29	3.95
_____	FOGLIO, FRANK—Hey God!	TA27	3.95
_____	FREEMAN, HOBART—Angels of Light?	TA10	3.95
_____	FROST, ROBERT—Aglow With The Spirit	TA15	3.95
_____	HARPER, MICHAEL—Walk in The Spirit	TA8X	3.95
_____	JARMAN, Ray—Pseudo Christians	TA7X	3.95
_____	KATZ, ARTHUR—Ben Israel	TA4X	3.95
_____	KUHLMAN, KATHRYN—Hour with Kuhlman	TA18	3.95
_____	MUMFORD, BOB—15 Steps Out	TA9X	3.95
_____	ORSINI, FR. JOSEPH—Hear My Confession	TA23	3.95
_____	PRANGE, ERVIN—The Gift Is Already Yours	TA33	3.95
_____	RANAGAHAN, KEVIN—Catholic Pentecostals	TA19	3.95
_____	ROBERTSON, PAT—Shout It from the Housetop	TA25	3.95
_____	SAINT, PHIL—Amazing Saints	TA24	3.95
_____	SANFORD, AGNES—Sealed Orders	TA35	3.95
_____	SIMPSON, CHARLES—So. Bapt. Looks At Pentecost	TA20	3.95
_____	SMITH, MALCOLM—Turn Your Back on the Prob.	TA26	3.95
_____	STREETER, PHIL—Ireland's Hope	TA32	3.95

PRICE SUBJECT TO CHANGE WITHOUT NOTICE

____	**TOMCZAK, LARRY**—Clap Your Hands	TA36	3.95
____	**WALLACE, WENDELL**—Born to Burn	TA12	3.95
____	**WARNKE, MIKE**—The Satan Seller	TA28	3.95
____	**WHITE, CLINTON**—From the Belly of the Whale	TA14	3.95
____	**WILLIAMS, J. RODMAN**—Era of the Spirit	TA16	3.95
____	**NEW TESTAMENT**—Steven B. Stevens (FIFTEEN TAPES)	NTCL	69.95

_____   TOTAL   _____

order from your local bookstore or

> Wholesale Book Sales
> Box 292
> Watchung, N.J. 07061

PRICE SUBJECT TO CHANGE WITHOUT NOTICE

SUGGESTED INEXPENSIVE PAPERBACK BOOKS
. . . WHEREVER PAPERBACKS ARE SOLD
OR USE HANDY ORDER FORM.

QUANTITY

	Title	Code	Price
____	AGLOW WITH THE SPIRIT—Frost	L326	.95
____	AMAZING SAINTS—Saint	L409	2.50
____	AND FORBID NOT TO SPEAK—Ervin	L329	.95
____	AND SIGNS FOLLOWED—Price	P002	1.50
____	ANGLES OF LIGHT?—Freeman	A506	.95
____	ANSWERS TO PRAISE—Carothers	L670	1.95
____	ANVIL—Orsini	P089	1.25
____	ARMSTRONG ERROR—DeLoach	L317	.95
____	AS AT THE BEGINNING—Harper	L721	.95
____	BAPTISM IN THE SPIRIT—Schep	L343	1.50
____	BAPTISM IN THE SPIRIT—BIBLICAL —Cockburn	16F	.65
____	BAPTISM OF FIRE—Harper	8F	.60
____	BAPTIZED IN ONE SPIRIT—Baker	1F	.60
____	BAPTIZED IN THE SPIRIT—Clark	P9	.75
____	BEN ISRAEL—Katz	A309	.95
____	BLACK TRACKS—Miles	A298	.95
____	BLESS YOUR DIRTY HEART—Lindsey	P017	1.95
____	BORN TO BURN—Wallace	A508	.95
____	CATHOLIC PENTECOSTALISM—McDonnell	P6	.60
____	CHALLENGING COUNTERFEIT—Gasson	L102	.95
____	CLAP YOUR HANDS—Tomczak	P073	2.50
____	COMING ALIVE—Buckingham	A501	.95
____	CONCISE GOSPELS AND ACTS —Christianson	P008	2.50
____	CONFESSIONS OF A HERETIC—Hunt	L31X	2.50
____	COUNSELOR TO COUNSELOR—Campbell	L335	1.50
____	DAYSPRING—White	L334	1.95
____	DAY THE DOLLAR DIES—Cantelon	P013	2.50
____	DISCOVERY (Booklet)—Frost	F71X	.50
____	DIVINE HEALING—Murray	P080	1.25
____	DO YOURSELF A FAVOR—Williams	P055	2.50
____	ERA OF THE SPIRIT—Williams	L322	1.95
____	FIFTEEN STEPS OUT—Mumford	L106	1.50
____	FROM THE BELLY OF THE WHALE—White	A318	.95
____	FULL BLESSING OF PENTECOST—Murray	P061	1.25
____	GATHERED FOR POWER—Pulkingham	MB1X	2.50
____	GIFT IS ALREADY YOURS—Prange	P037	2.50

PRICE SUBJECT TO CHANGE WITHOUT NOTICE

_____	GLAD YOU ASKED THAT—R. Bennett	P084	2.50
_____	GOD BREAKS IN—Congdon	L313	1.95
_____	GOD DID NOT ORDAIN SILENCE —Christianson	P054	2.50
_____	GOD IS FOR THE EMOTIONALLY ILL —Guldseth	A507	.95
_____	GOD'S JUNKIE—Arguinzoni	A509	.95
_____	GOD'S LIVING ROOM—Walker	A123	.95
_____	GONE IS SHADOWS' CHILD—Foy	L337	.95
_____	GRACE AND THE GLORY OF GOD —Benson/Jarman	L104	1.50
_____	HEALING ADVENTURE—White	L345	1.95
_____	HEALING LIGHT—Sanford	L726	.95
_____	HEAR MY CONFESSION—Orsini	L341	1.00
_____	HEY GOD!—Foglio	P007	1.95
_____	HOLY LAND HYMNS—Brumback	P087	1.45
_____	HOLY SPIRIT AND YOU—Bennett	L324	2.50
_____	IN THE SECRET PLACE—Van Woerdan	P081	1.25
_____	IRELAND'S HOPE—Streeter	P027	1.25
_____	JESUS AND ISRAEL—Benson	A514	.95
_____	JESUS CHRIST UNIVERSITY—Summers	P051	.95
_____	JESUS PEOPLE ARE COMING—King	A519	.95
_____	KINGDOM OF DARKNESS—Thomas	P034	1.95
_____	KINGDOM OF SELF—Jabay	P062	2.50
_____	LAYMAN'S COMMENTARY HOLY SPIRIT—Rea	P014	2.50
_____	LET THIS CHURCH DIE—Weaver	A520	.95
_____	LET US PRAISE—Cornwall	P039	2.50
_____	LEWI PETHRUS: SPIRITUAL MEMOIR —Pethrus	P043	1.95
_____	LIFE IN THE HOLY SPIRIT—Harper	5F	.50
_____	LIVING PROMISES—Summers	P986	1.25
_____	LONELY NOW—Cruz	A510	1.25
_____	LORD OF THE VALLEYS—Bulle	L018	2.50
_____	LOST SHEPHERD—Sanford	L328	.95
_____	MADE ALIVE—Price	P001	1.50
_____	MANIFEST VICTORY—Moseley	L724	2.50
_____	MANNERS AND CUSTOMS OF BIBLE —Freeman	P022	2.95
_____	MICHAEL, MICHAEL—Esses	P047	2.50
_____	MIRACLES THROUGH PRAYER—Harrell	A518	.95
_____	MY KID'S ON DRUGS—Watson	P067	1.25
_____	NEW TESTAMENT CHURCH BOOK—West	P045	1.95
_____	NEW WAY OF LIVING—Harper	P066	2.50

PRICE SUBJECT TO CHANGE WITHOUT NOTICE

	Title	Code	Price
_____	NICKY CRUZ GIVES THE FACTS ON DRUGS —Cruz	B70	.50
_____	NINE O'CLOCK IN THE MORNING—Bennett	P555	2.50
_____	NOAH'S ARK—I TOUCHED IT—Navarra	P065	2.95
_____	NONE CAN GUESS—Harper	L722	1.95
_____	OUT OF THIS WORLD—Fisher	A517	.95
_____	OVERFLOWING LIFE—Frost	P050	2.50
_____	PASTOR'S WIFE—Wurmbrand	P032	2.50
_____	PATHWAY TO POWER—Davison	L00X	1.50
_____	PENTECOST BEHIND IRON CURTAIN —Durasoff	P018	1.50
_____	PENTECOST IN THE CATHOLIC CHURCH —O'Connor	P8	.60
_____	PENTECOSTAL REALITY—Williams	P016	1.50
_____	PENTECOSTALS—Nichol	L711	2.50
_____	PHENOMENON OF OBEDIENCE—Esses	P085	2.50
_____	PIONEERS OF REVIVAL—Clarke	L723	.95
_____	POWER IN PRAISE—Carothers	L342	1.95
_____	POWER FOR THE BODY—Harper	4F	.85
_____	PRAISE WORKS!—Carothers	P060	1.95
_____	PRAYER MEETINGS—Cavnar	P2	.50
_____	PREACHER WITH A BILLY CLUB—Asmuth	A209	.95
_____	PRISON TO PRAISE—Carothers	A504	1.25
_____	PROPHECY: A GIFT FOR THE BODY—Harper	2FXX	.65
_____	PSEUDO CHRISTIANS—Jarman	A516	.95
_____	REAL FAITH—Price	P000	1.50
_____	REMARKABLE MIRACLES—Bevington	P063	2.50
_____	RISE TO NEWNESS OF LIFE—Beal	EP01	2.95
_____	RUN BABY RUN—Cruz	L101	.95
_____	RUN BABY RUN—Cruz (ComicBook)		.25
_____	SATAN SELLER—Warnke	L794	2.50
_____	SEEDS OF CONFLICT—DeLoach	P077	2.50
_____	SET MY SPIRIT FREE—Frost	P058	2.50
_____	SOUL PATROL—Bartlett	A500	.95
_____	SPEAKING WITH GOD—Cantelon	L336	.95
_____	SPIRIT BADE ME GO—duPlessis	L325	.95
_____	SPIRITUAL AND PHYSICAL HEALTH—Price	P003	1.95
_____	SPIRITUAL GIFTS—Clark	P3	.50
_____	SPIRITUAL WARFARE—Harper	A505	.95
_____	STRONGER THAN PRISON WALLS—Wurmbrand	A956	.95
_____	SUPERNATURAL DREAMS AND VISIONS	L304	2.95
_____	TAKE ANOTHER LOOK—Mumford	L338	2.50
_____	THERE'S MORE—Hall	L344	1.50
_____	THESE ARE NOT DRUNKEN—Ervin	L105	2.50

PRICE SUBJECT TO CHANGE WITHOUT NOTICE

QUANTITY

_____	THEY LEFT THEIR NETS—Pulkingham	PM02	2.50
_____	THIS EARTH'S END—Benson	A513	.95
_____	THIS WHICH YE SEE AND HEAR—Ervin	L728	1.95
_____	TONGUES UNDER FIRE—Lillie	3F	.85
_____	TURN YOUR BACK ON THE PROBLEM—Smith	L034	1.95
_____	TWO WORLDS—Price	P004	1.95
_____	UNDERGROUND SAINTS—Wurmbrand	U1	.95
_____	WALK IN THE SPIRIT—Harper	L319	.95
_____	WE'VE BEEN ROBBED—Meloon	L339	1.50
_____	WHAT WILL SIMON SAY—McGinnis	P075	2.50
_____	YOU CAN KNOW GOD—Price	P005	.75
_____	YOUNG LIONS OF JUDAH—Evans	P059	1.25
_____	YOUR NEW LOOK—Buckingham	A503	.95
_____	YOUTH WITH A MISSION—Wilson	A152	.95
_____	TOTAL		_____

Books listed above are available wherever religious paperbacks are sold
—or order directly from:

Wholesale Book Sales
Box 292
Watchung, N.J. 07061

───────── **ORDER FORM** ─────────

Please send Inspirational Books checked above—Cash, Check or
Money order must be enclosed—books will be shipped free.

TOTAL OF BOOKS ORDERED   _____

TOTAL AMOUNT DUE   _____
(Books shipped free)

NAME _____

STREET _____

CITY _____ STATE _____ ZIP _____

PRICE SUBJECT TO CHANGE WITHOUT NOTICE

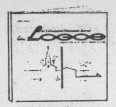

FREE
SAMPLE COPY
OF
LOGOS

An International Magazine of New Testament Christianity

Worldwide coverage of Religious News
Book Reviews
Trends and Current Issues
Feature Articles by such Internationally
  known writers as:

James Lee Beal	Irene Burk	Pat Robertson
Dennis Bennett	Harrell	Agnes Sanford
Harold Bredesen	Arthur Katz	Malcolm Smith
Jamie	Kathryn Kuhlman	Cardinal Suenens
Buckingham	Mrs. Gordon	Corrie TenBoom
Larry Christenson	Lindsay	Tommy Tyson
Nicky Cruz	Dan Malachuk	William
David duPlessis	Peter Marshall	Willoughby
Betty Lee Esses	Bob Mumford	Al West
Frank Foglio	Father Joseph	J. Rodman
Dr. Robert Frost	Orsini	Williams
Michael Harper	Derek Prince	

☐ Send
Complete
Catalogue

☐ Sample
copy of the
LOGOS JOURNAL

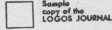

Order blank on previous page